DOS 6

A Tutorial to Accompany
Peter Norton's Introduction to Computers

Terrence P. O'Donnell

GLENCOE
McGraw-Hill

New York, New York   Columbus, Ohio   Woodland Hills, California   Peoria, Illinois

Library of Congress Cataloging-in-Publication Data

O'Donnell, Terrence P., 1959–
    DOS 6: A Tutorial to Accompany Peter Norton's Introduction to
    Computers / Terrence Patrick O'Donnell.
    p. cm.
    Includes index.
    ISBN 0-02-801328-X
    1. MS-DOS (Computer file)   2. PC-DOS (Computer file)   I. Norton,
Peter, 1943–   Introduction to computers.   II. Title.
QA76.76.0630343   1994   93-44147
005.4'469—dc20   CIP

Concept, Development, and Production: BMR, Corte Madera, Ca.

DOS 6: A Tutorial to Accompany Peter Norton's Introduction to Computers

Send all inquiries to:
Glencoe/McGraw-Hill
936 Eastwind Drive
Westerville, OH 43081

ISBN 0-02-801328-X

6 7 8 9 10   005   01 00 99 98

MS-DOS is a registered trademark of Microsoft Corporation.

CONTENTS

PREFACE

This *DOS 6 Tutorial* is only one of the instructional tools that complement *Peter Norton's Introduction to Computers*. Glencoe and Peter Norton have teamed up to provide a new approach to computer education, one not reflected in traditional computer textbooks. The text and its ancillary materials are grounded in the philosophy that it is knowledgeable and empowered end users who will provide the gains in productivity that both businesses and individuals need to achieve in the 1990's and beyond. The skills that students develop through applied practice will translate into more effective and efficient computer use, whether at home or in the workplace.

The Role of DOS in the Computer World

DOS is the most widely used operating system for IBM and IBM-compatible personal computers, which predominate business, social, and educational institutions. Learning to use the basic functions of DOS is the obvious starting point for many end users, who recognize the important role DOS plays in managing the operation of, and interrelationship between, the hardware and applications software. For students wishing to learn how to use personal computers most effectively and efficiently, learning to use basic DOS commands can help demystify the computer's operation.

In this tutorial students will learn how to manage data and manipulate the operating system effectively; they will gain a better understanding of an operating system's function. Students will learn valuable data management skills and helpful problem-solving techniques.

How to Use This Tutorial

Because using DOS commands is critical to understanding how to use the computer effectively, it is helpful for students to obtain a good understanding of the concepts presented in *Peter Norton's Introduction to Computers* before proceeding with the tutorial. However, students can use the tutorial as they explore and expand their initial understanding of computers and their many uses.

This DOS tutorial contains two lessons that are structured in modular format. A general topic, such as creating subdirectories on a disk, is covered in a brief but comprehensive overview. Following the overview, a series of numbered steps guide the student through the application of relevant commands to achieve a particular result related to the topic.

Each succeeding topic then builds, wherever practical, on the preceding topic to reinforce skills as the student progresses through the applied operations. Each lesson concludes with a battery of review questions and additional applications that reinforce conceptual discussion and applied practice.

Other Instructional Support

To provide instructors with additional resources for administering their courses, Glencoe has developed an innovative *Instructor's Productivity Center (IPC)*. The *IPC* contains not only the computerized testbank, but also files from the *Instructor's Manual and Key*, electronic transparencies, Peter Norton newsletter updates, and student data files that correspond to the innovative "Exploring Your Computer" section—hands-on exercises at the end of the main text.

The *DOS 6 Tutorial* also has its own *Instructor's Manual and Key*, with hints and teaching tips, lecture outlines, answers to end-of-lesson questions, and additional application projects.

LESSON 1   GETTING ACQUAINTED WITH MS-DOS

Objectives

After completing this lesson, you will be able to do the following:

- Understand the functions of an operating system.
- Understand MS-DOS versions, release numbers, and upward compatibility.
- Recognize data disks as media for storing electronic data, and identify disk drive configurations for personal computers.
- Boot up MS-DOS software on a personal computer.
- Change the current disk drive.
- Understand MS-DOS rules for naming files.
- Enter commands at the DOS prompt.
- Distinguish between internal and external DOS commands.
- Use the internal DOS command CLS to clear the screen.
- Use the external DOS command FORMAT.COM command to format a blank diskette.
- Use the internal DOS commands MD, CD, and RD to create, make current, and delete subdirectories, respectively.
- Use the internal DIR command to display a directory list for the current subdirectory.
- Define path names and file specifications.

The operation of a personal computer requires interaction between its hardware components, applications software, and, most importantly, you the user. In this tutorial you will get acquainted with MS-DOS 6.0, the software that manages this interaction for efficient operation of an IBM or IBM-compatible personal computer. This lesson will introduce you to the basics of operating systems, and to MS-DOS operations that will help you to manage files and work effectively with a personal computer.

Basic Operating System Functions

An **operating system** is a set of computer programs that controls the computer's operation and manages the operating environment. The **operating environment** consists of the user, the computer's hardware, peripheral devices (other hardware devices that are connected to the computer, such as monitors and printers), and applications software. A **peripheral device** is any machine that is not a physical part of the computer but operates in combination with it.

1

Operating system software is different from applications software. **Applications software** are sets of programs designed for specific or custom purposes. Consider the following examples of common applications software:

- Word processing software facilitates the use of the written word to compose and edit all kinds of documents.

- Spreadsheet software provides arithmetic formulas to perform numerical calculations to create budgets, project financial plans, or solve quantitative problems.

- Database software allows for managing, organizing, and storing related sets of information.

- Desktop publishing software supplies a graphic environment for designing pages.

- Communications software expedites information transfer to other locations via telephone lines.

- Graphics software permits freehand rendering of visual objects and illustrations.

These types of applications are just six examples of the many software products people use with personal computers. Applications software products are, essentially, tools. They are specially designed tools that interact with a computer's operating system software to help a user perform specific tasks.

To illustrate the details of this interaction in a practical situation, think about the process of using a personal computer and a word processing application to write a letter. As soon as you turn on the computer, the operating system goes to work setting up the working environment. Next, you enter a command that the operating system uses to start the word processing program. Then, the word processing program continues to interact with the operating system while you type, edit, format, and save your letter on disk. Finally, you and the word processing software communicate with the operating system so that it successfully locates the file on the disk drive that stores the letter and sends the file's data to the printer, which is connected to the computer. Then the printer prints your letter.

Sometimes, you must interact directly with the operating system software. For example, when you issue commands that cause the computer to display information about the system environment or to list files stored on a disk, you are interacting directly with the operating system.

The Importance of the Operating System

An operating system—any operating system—is vital to the operation of a computer for the following reasons:

- An operating system establishes the character and environment in which the user and programs interact with the computer.

- Along with the personal computer's hardware, an operating system defines and establishes the practical limits of the system's usefulness.

- An operating system brings a computer—an otherwise inanimate object—to "life."

- An operating system permits the operation of only those programs that were written specifically to work with it and the type of computer for which it was designed.

- The skills acquired through using a specific (and well-designed) operating system remain valid for using its updated versions or even other operating systems.

The Operating System for the Family of IBM Personal Computers

DOS is the name of the operating system developed by Microsoft Corporation for the IBM PC and all IBM-compatible personal computers. **DOS** stands for **disk operating system**. The company, International Business Machines (IBM), refers to the operating systems it distributes for its personal computer and PS/2 product lines as **PC-DOS** or **IBM DOS**. **MS-DOS** (short for Microsoft-DOS) is the operating system distributed by Microsoft Corporation for the many IBM-compatible personal computers that are manufactured by other companies. For most users, there is very little difference between the operation of MS-DOS, PC-DOS, and IBM DOS.

DOS Versions and Upward Compatibility

All versions and releases of DOS are indicated by a number, for example, MS-DOS 6.0. The first number refers to the version and the number after the decimal refers to the release of a particular version. In general terms, a new version represents a significant update or improvement over the earlier version. A new release on the other hand, represents changes or programming fixes for the current version. For example, DOS 3.1 modified DOS 3.0 by providing for data transfer with the new high-density 5.25-inch diskettes that were introduced for personal computers in 1984.

MS-DOS 6.0, released in April 1993, is Microsoft Corporation's latest version of operating system software for IBM-compatible personal computers. In addition to supporting all features associated with MS-DOS 5.0 and earlier, MS-DOS 6.0 includes many significant new features. Some of these features will be discussed later in this tutorial.

Storing Information on Data Disks

The movement of data between the computer's components is one of the most important functions of an operating system—hence the acronym, "disk operating system." Data is entered, processed within, and exits the computer system in electronic form. To handle and move the data properly during these operations, the computer must be equipped with one or more storage devices. A **storage device** receives data electronically, holds it for an indefinite period, and then supplies it upon command when you (and the computer) need it. Data can be stored on various types of disks. **Disks** are, in general, round objects with a magnetic coating; they store the electronic impulses that make up the data.

Storing Data on Diskettes

Diskettes (sometimes called floppy disks) are very thin platters that are encased in either a soft (flexible) or hard plastic jacket. Diskettes are storage devices that allow data to be transported from one computer to another. They are also very useful for backing up data that is stored on a hard disk drive in case the hard disk drive crashes and loses its data.

Size	Storage Capacity	Density	
3.5 inch	720KB	double	**Table 1-1**
3.5 inch	1.44MB	high	
3.5 inch	2.88MB	high	Diskette Types, Sizes, and Recording Densities
5.25 inch	360KB	double	
5.25 inch	1.2MB	high	

There are several types of diskettes; they vary in size and storage capacity, or recording density (the amount of data, in bytes, that the disk can store). Table 1-1 lists the different types of diskettes in common use.

Diskettes can be categorized either as double density or high density. How can you tell if a diskette has double-density or high-density capacity? Some manufacturers label 5.25-inch diskettes with their capacities. However, if you find that you cannot tell the capacity of an unlabeled, blank diskette, examine the hub ring in its center. Double-density diskettes have a dark or colored hub ring, while high-density diskettes have no apparent hub ring.

You can tell a 3.5-inch diskette's capacity by checking the top edge of its hard plastic jacket or cover for the number of square, write-protect holes or windows, as shown in Figure 1-1. A double-density diskette has only one write-protect window in the upper-right corner when looking at the top of the diskette. High-density diskettes have a write-protect window in the upper-right corner of the diskette and another square hole in the upper-left corner. The top side of a diskette is the side that does *not* show the disk's round, metal hub, which you can see when you look at the back side of the diskette. The top side is the side that is face up when you insert the diskette into a disk drive.

Write-Protecting Diskettes

All diskettes can be write-protected, which means the data stored on the diskette can be protected from being erased or overwritten by other data. In all types of 3.5-inch diskettes there is a little door that slides up and down in the upper-right corner write-protect window.

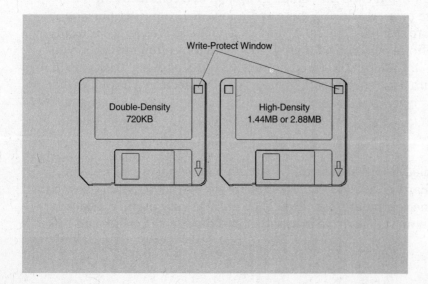

Figure 1-1

Double-density 3.5-inch (720KB) diskettes have a single write-protect window on the diskette's upper-right corner. High-density 3.5-inch (1.44 and 2.88MB) diskettes have a second hole in their upper-left corners, in addition to the write-protect window.

When the door is open—that is, when you can see through the window—the computer can write data to the disk. However, when you slide the door up to close the window—that is, you cannot see through it—then data cannot be written to the disk. Data can be read from the disk only when the little sliding door covers the write-protect window.

On 5.25-inch diskettes, there is a write-protect notch on the right edge of the soft plastic jacket when you are looking at the top side of the diskette. The diskette can be write-protected by folding a piece of tape (or one of the write-protect tabs that are packaged with diskettes) over both sides of the notch so that the notch is covered.

Storing Data on Hard Disk Drives

Hard disks in hard (or fixed) disk drives are similar to plastic diskettes except that they are made of metal and reside within a sealed housing that can be either removable or mounted inside the computer. Hard disks have much higher storage capacities than diskettes. They are best used for storing the operating system's program files, applications programs, and frequently used data files. Hard disks have storage capacities that range from 10MB to sizes measured in gigabytes (1024MB equals one gigabyte).

Recognizing Disk Drive Configurations

A **disk drive configuration** refers to the types of disk drive devices with which a system is equipped. There are three common configurations:

- systems with a hard disk drive (also called a fixed disk) and at least one diskette drive
- systems with one or two diskette drives and no hard disk drive
- systems connected to other computer systems via a local area network (LAN)

The devices that make up these configurations are discussed in more detail in the following sections.

Using Diskette Drives

Diskette drives, or floppy disk drives, are input/output devices that facilitate the use of diskettes for reading and writing information. An **input/output (I/O) device** is a peripheral device that sends and/or receives the data that the computer works with either by reading the data from or writing the data to the diskette. The data is read or written via the device's read/write head—a magnetic component that barely clears the disk's surface as the disk spins beneath it. In terms of its operation, the read/write head's function is comparable to the recording head in a tape recorder or a video cartridge recorder (VCR).

There are several types of disk drives that read data from and write data to diskettes. The most important aspect to be aware of is whether the disk drive can accommodate high-density diskettes. For instance, some 5.25-inch disk drives can read only double-density (360KB) diskettes and cannot be used for high-density (1.2MB) diskettes. These disk drive types are, however, fast becoming obsolete. Note that disk drives that do accommodate high-density diskettes also can accommodate double-density diskettes.

A disk drive has a **drive name**, which is a single letter that distinguishes it from the other disk drives in the system. Typically, the drive name A identifies the single diskette drive in a system that is also equipped with a hard disk drive. If a system (with or without a hard disk drive) is equipped with two disk drives, the left or top drive is called drive A and the right or bottom drive is called drive B.

Using Hard Disk Drives

Hard disk drives can be removable or mounted (fixed) inside the computer's hardware. They house the disk(s) and the read/write head(s) together. Hard disks typically have the drive name C. Sometimes hard disk space is **partitioned** to function as two or more separate drives, even though it is a single unit. Typically, such hard disks have two or three partitions; the first partition is called drive C, the second drive D, and the third (if applicable), drive E.

Using File Servers on Local Area Networks (LANs)

Local Area Networks (LANs) are series of personal computers that are connected so they can share data. One of the computers is called a **file server**. This computer contains a high-capacity hard disk drive that stores applications programs and data files that can be accessed by any of the connected computers. Commonly, the file server drive is called drive F. Computers connected to the LAN can be equipped with a single diskette drive, drive A, at the very least and, more likely, a hard disk drive as well (drive C).

Starting a Personal Computer

To begin using a personal computer you must turn it on. Then DOS must be loaded into random access memory (RAM), the system's main memory. The manner in which this takes place depends on the type of disk configuration in the system. There are also two methods for loading the operating system, depending on whether power to the computer has been switched on.

Booting DOS

Loading DOS into random access memory (RAM) is a process called **booting**. The term "booting" derives from the expression "to pull (something) up by its bootstraps." When a personal computer is switched on and the operating system is booted, essentially a two-step process occurs. First, a small program built into a chip on the computer's **motherboard**, or **system board**, performs a self-test routine to make sure all is well with the system. Second, another built-in start-up program, generally referred to as a **bootstrap loader**, is programmed to read the first part of a disk. This area of the disk, which can be either a hard disk or a diskette, contains the DOS program files that hold special DOS instructions that set up the operating system and load it into the computer's RAM.

Performing a Cold Boot to Load DOS

You perform a cold boot by switching on electrical power to a personal computer that has been turned off. Power to the system initiates the simple, built-in start-up programs that check the system and boot DOS.

Booting DOS with a Hard Disk Configuration

If the computer is equipped with a hard disk, then the DOS program files are installed on this disk. Switching on the power will cause the bootstrap loader program to read the first part of the hard disk that contains the DOS loading instructions. The process takes a few moments. Once DOS is loaded, some system status messages display, and then the DOS prompt appears. The **DOS prompt** displays the active, or current, drive name (for example, C:\>). To the right of the greater-than sign (>) is a flashing cursor, which indicates the position where the next character will display when a user begins typing characters at the keyboard. When you see a DOS prompt, MS-DOS is ready to receive commands.

Booting DOS with a Diskette Drive

Although they are becoming obsolete, it is possible for a computer to be equipped with either one or two diskette drives and no hard disk drive at all. For such a configuration, a diskette containing the essential MS-DOS program files must be used to boot DOS. This diskette, often referred to as the **system disk**, must be inserted into drive A *before* the power to the computer is switched on. When the power is switched on, the startup routine is initiated, and the bootstrap loader reads the first part of the DOS system disk in drive A for the loading instructions. With this type of disk configuration, the booting process will very likely require the user to enter the current date and time.

Entering the Current Date and Time

Nowadays, personal computers are commonly equipped with a battery that helps the system keep track of the current date and time during those times when the power to the computer is switched off. MS-DOS reads the current date and time information during the booting process, so after displaying some system status messages at startup, the DOS prompt appears and the operating system is ready to receive commands. Computers without hard disks, however, might not contain batteries. If this is the case, MS-DOS will display the following prompt in the upper-left corner of the screen during the booting process.

```
Current date is Tue 01-01-1980
Enter new date (mm-dd-yy):
```

Type the numbers for the date in the format indicated in the prompt. Valid numbers for the month are 1–12, and valid numbers for the day are 1–31. For the year numbers, you can enter two digits, 90–99, for the the current year through 1999; enter four digits for the years 2000–2099. After you type the numbers for the current date, press Enter. MS-DOS stores the current date, and then displays the following prompt.

```
Current time is 0:00:00.00
Enter new time:
```

Type the numbers for the current time. You need enter only the numbers for the hour and minutes separated by a colon (:); the value for seconds is optional. If you enter values corresponding to a 12-hour format (for example, 1:30 p.m.), type an **a** or a **p** to indicate a.m or p.m. However, you can also use the 24-hour format to indicate a.m or p.m.

(for example, 13:30 for 1:30 p.m.). Valid numbers for the hour are 1–23; valid numbers for minutes and seconds are 0–59. After you type the numbers for the current time, press [Enter]. MS-DOS stores the current time, and completes the booting process, displaying the DOS prompt (for example, A:\>).

Starting a Computer on a LAN

The process for switching on (and cold booting) a computer that is connected to a LAN configuration is very similar. If the computer is equipped with a hard disk, the special DOS instructions that load DOS into memory will most likely reside on the first part of the hard disk (sometimes called the local hard disk drive) that is in the computer. If the computer is equipped with one or two diskette drives and no hard disk, a DOS system disk may be necessary to cold boot the computer.

However, users of computers that are connected to a LAN may not have to perform any startup procedures. Often a knowledgeable supervisor or technician, whose responsibilities include supervision, maintenance, and troubleshooting of the networked system, takes care of startup procedures, including properly starting the network's file server. Although procedures vary, depending on the network software, it is very likely that any computer in a LAN configuration will include special startup instructions that automatically "log" the computer into the network when the power is switched on. If in doubt about starting a computer that is connected to a LAN, consult the system's supervisor or technician.

Performing a Warm Boot to Start DOS

Sometimes MS-DOS must be reloaded, or reset, on a computer that already has its power switched on. This is known as a **warm boot**. You perform a warm boot by pressing three keys simultaneously. To press multiple keys on a computer keyboard simultaneously, you press and hold down the one or more keys, press the last key, and then release all the keys at the same time. Often this is necessary for two keys only. However, when you perform a warm boot, you must press three keys in this manner: the Control key ([Ctrl]), the Alternate key ([Alt]), and the Delete key ([Del]). To perform a warm boot, press and hold down [Ctrl] and [Alt] simultaneously with your left hand, press [Del] with your right hand, and then release all three keys at the same time. In this tutorial, keys to be pressed in this manner are shown connected with hyphens, for example, [Ctrl]-[Alt]-[Del].

If the computer on which DOS is being warm booted is equipped with a hard disk, the DOS instructions for loading DOS into memory are read again from the first part of the disk. If the computer is equipped with one or two diskette drives and no hard disk drive, the system disk (the diskette containing essential MS-DOS information) must be inserted into drive A before pressing [Ctrl]-[Alt]-[Del].

The following exercise is your first guided activity in which you will practice applying some of the concepts and operations discussed above. The steps in these sections will apply to hard disk configuration users primarily. Users of systems without a hard disk, however, can apply the steps successfully for practice within their disk configurations. Throughout this tutorial, steps applicable to diskette drive configurations will be listed separately wherever the application requires separate procedures.

Boot DOS

Now you will begin to learn about the operating system by starting your computer, if necessary, and booting DOS.

Hard Disk Drive Systems:

1. If the computer you are using is switched off, turn it on by flipping its power switch to the ON position. If the computer's power is already switched on, go to step 3.

2. If the computer's monitor has a separate power switch, make sure it is switched to the ON position.

   After a few moments, some status messages display followed by the DOS prompt C:\>, as shown in Figure 1-2.

3. If the computer you are using is switched on, press Ctrl-Alt-Del to perform a warm boot.

   After MS-DOS is reloaded, a DOS prompt displays.

Diskette Drive Systems:

1. Place a DOS system disk in drive A.

2. If the computer you are using is switched off, turn it on by flipping its power switch to the ON position. If the computer's power is already switched on, go to step 6.

3. If the computer's monitor has a separate power switch, make sure it is switched to the ON position.

4. If a message asking you to enter the current date displays, type the value that corresponds to the current date and press Enter.

5. If a message asking you to enter the current time displays, type the value that corresponds to the current time and press Enter.

   After a few moments, some status messages display followed by the DOS prompt A:\>.

Figure 1-2

The DOS prompt displays after MS-DOS is booted by the personal computer. The DOS prompt means that MS-DOS is ready to receive commands from the user.

```
C:\>
```

6. If the computer you are using is switched on, press Ctrl-Alt-Del to perform a warm boot.

   After MS-DOS is reloaded, a DOS prompt displays.

Understanding the DOS Prompt

The DOS prompt is where you enter commands for MS-DOS operations or startup applications programs. The DOS prompt displays the current drive name. After startup, the current drive is the drive that contains the disk that stores DOS files. So if DOS booted from drive C (the hard disk), then the DOS prompt C:\> indicates that drive C is the current disk drive. Likewise, if DOS boots from a system disk in drive A, then the DOS prompt A:\> indicates that drive A is current.

Using the Current Disk Drive

To the immediate right of the DOS prompt is a flashing cursor. Any character you type will display at the cursor's position as soon as you press its corresponding key on the keyboard. The cursor displays to the right of the character, indicating the position where the next character you type will display. Commands or program names that are stored on the disk in the active drive can be executed simply by typing the command, or the program name, and then pressing Enter.

Changing the Current Drive

The current drive can be changed at any time. To do this, you simply type the drive name letter, followed by a colon (for example, a: or A:), and press Enter. Together the drive letter and colon (:) form the **drive specification**. When you enter a drive specification for another disk drive, a new DOS prompt displays below the previous DOS prompt. The new DOS prompt's drive name reflects the new current drive, as shown in Figure 1-3. Before you enter a drive specification for a diskette drive, there must be a diskette that is formatted appropriately properly inserted into that drive. Disk formatting will be discussed later in this lesson.

```
C:\>a:

A:\>
```

Figure 1-3

When you enter a drive specification, MS-DOS makes the drive you specify the current disk drive.

Change the Current Disk Drive

Now, you will practice changing the current disk drive. If you are using a system that is equipped with two diskette drives and no hard drive, substitute drive B for drive A and drive A for drive C in any of the following numbered instructions.

1. Make sure your computer is switched on and that the system has booted MS-DOS properly.

2. Insert a properly formatted diskette into drive A (or drive B if your system does not have a hard disk drive). See your instructor for a properly formatted diskette.

3. Type **a:** and press (Enter).

   The drive name you specified is now the current drive.

4. Type **c:** and press (Enter) (or type **a:** if drive A contains the MS-DOS system disk).

   The drive name you specified is current.

Entering DOS Commands

Any command you enter at the DOS prompt can be typed in either uppercase, lowercase, or any combination of upper- and lowercase characters. DOS makes no distinction between upper- and lowercase. As you have seen, after typing the exact characters that make up a command or program name, you "enter" the command by pressing the (Enter) key. You will soon learn to use a variety of DOS commands. Some DOS commands return status information; others perform tasks or functions.

Correcting Typing Mistakes

When typing commands at the DOS prompt, it is common to make frequent typing mistakes. If you make a typing mistake before you press (Enter), simply press (Bksp) as many times as is necessary to clear the incorrect characters, and then retype. If the command is long and contains several errors, you can obtain a new DOS prompt by pressing (Esc) and then pressing (Enter). Then simply type the command again.

If the command is not typed correctly and you press (Enter) to execute the command, DOS will very likely display the following message:

```
Bad command or file name
```

Below the message another DOS prompt will display. Simply retype the command at the new prompt and press (Enter).

Understanding File Names

In the DOS environment there are primarily two types of files: data files and program files. **Data files** store sets of data a user creates when using an applications program. For instance, when using a word processing program, you can save a document, such as a letter or a report, in a data file. **Program files**, on the other hand, contain characters in a specific arrangement that forms programming instructions. These instructions command the computer to perform one or more specific tasks. A program can be an operating system program (a DOS file); an applications program, such as a spreadsheet or database program; or a special set of instructions written in a language the computer uses to perform customized tasks.

Understanding File Name Rules

All files, data files and program files, are identified by a name called a **file name**. A file name has two parts: the filename and the extension. A **filename** is any name composed of between one and eight characters for the file. An **extension** is an additional one-to-three character extension to the filename that is separated from the filename by a period (.). Together these two elements make up what is termed a **file specification** (for example, FILE-NAME.EXT). File specifications will be discussed in greater detail later in this lesson.

The following rules for naming files must be followed for all files created in the MS-DOS environment:

1. Filenames and extensions can include the following characters:
    - alphabet letters A–Z
    - digits 0–9
    - ~ tilde
    - ! exclamation point
    - # pound sign
    - $ dollar sign
    - % percent sign
    - ^ caret
    - & ampersand
    - ( ) opening and closing parentheses
    - - hyphen
    - { } opening and closing braces
    - _ underscore

2. Filenames and extensions cannot include spaces.

3. The following symbols are reserved for other MS-DOS uses and *cannot* be used in file names:
    - * asterisk
    - + plus sign
    - = equals sign
    - [ ] opening/closing square brackets
    - " quote mark
    - ' apostrophe
    - ; semicolon

- ? question mark
- . period
- : colon
- / forward slash
- \ backslash
- | vertical split bar
- > greater-than sign
- < less-than sign

4. Do not use DOS device names as names for data or program files. Table 1-2 lists device names that DOS reserves. These are names, much like file names, that DOS uses to identify other components within the system.

Name	Device
AUX	(see COM1)
CLOCK$	system clock driver
COM1	serial communications line 1
COM2	serial communications line 2
COM3	serial communications line 3
COM4	serial communications line 4
CON	console (i.e., keyboard and monitor screen)
LPT1	parallel printer line 1
LPT2	parallel printer line 2
LPT3	parallel printer line 3
NUL	empty (data throw-away) file
PRN	(see LPT1)

Table 1-2

Device Names
Reserved by
MS-DOS

Distinguishing Between Data and Program Files

File name extensions are very useful for categorizing or classifying files by type. Basically, they fall into two categories: those that are used or assigned automatically by applications programs and those that you assign. For example, Microsoft Word, a word processing program, automatically assigns the file name extension DOC to document files that the user creates while working with the program. Lotus 1-2-3, a popular spreadsheet program, assigns the file name extension WK1 to any worksheet file created with its software releases 2.0, 2.01, 2.2, 2.3, and 2.4.

In the DOS environment, the file name extensions COM, BAT, EXE, and SYS identify files that fit into specific categories. Files with the COM and EXE extensions indicate executable files or commands. **Executable** files are written in special programming languages and perform one or more specific tasks when you enter the filename portion at the DOS prompt. For example, the file 123.EXE loads and runs the Lotus 1-2-3 program when you type 123 at the DOS prompt and press (Enter).

Files with the SYS extension are special system files that store hardware data or programs. The BAT extension refers to batch files. Batch files are used to store a series of commands, like those you can enter at the DOS prompt, that execute automatically one after the other when the batch filename is entered at the DOS prompt. When you create your own data or program files, avoid using the BAT, COM, EXE, and SYS file name extensions, unless they are appropriate for the data you are creating.

Like filenames, you are free to assign almost any file name extension that helps you to organize the data files or program files you create. Just stay aware of those extensions mentioned above that have special significance to MS-DOS, and avoid using them.

Understanding DOS Commands

As you know, **commands** are essentially filenames for program files. Consider the DOS file name PRINT.COM, for example. This file contains a program that sends data to the printer via a specific port, or connector device. For the time being, consider this file's filename simply as a command. Thus, when you enter the PRINT command, followed by some additional information that MS-DOS needs to execute the program properly, MS-DOS dutifully carries out the task following the instructions stored in the PRINT.COM file.

You can also type the file's extension (that is, PRINT.COM or print.com) when you enter the command, but it is not necessary to include the file name extension. The command will execute the program with or without the file name extension included.

Within MS-DOS there are two classifications for its commands: internal and external commands.

Using Internal Commands

Internal commands are commands that MS-DOS keeps resident in memory at all times, no matter what other tasks the computer is performing—i.e., running a custom program, running an applications program, or carrying out instructions in an MS-DOS program. A special, and very important, MS-DOS file called COMMAND.COM stores these internal commands. The COMMAND.COM file is sometimes referred to as a **command interpreter** because it is a program that displays the DOS prompt and waits for the user to enter commands. When the user does that, COMMAND.COM reads the command into memory and carries out its assigned instructions. If the command is an internal DOS command—for instance the COPY command, which copies a file from one disk location to another—COMMAND.COM executes a program that is stored in the COMMAND.COM program file to carry out the task. If the command is not an internal DOS command, COMMAND.COM looks elsewhere (on the current disk drive) for the program's filename.

Internal commands are programs that are used frequently, so they are always at your disposal when you work with a personal computer. And because they are built into the COMMAND.COM file, they occupy very little memory space so that you can use applications software. If MS-DOS tried to load all of its program files into memory, there would be no memory space left for other work.

Clearing the Screen with the CLS Command

The CLS command is another example of an internal DOS command. It is used to clear any information that currently displays on screen. After entering the CLS command, the DOS prompt displays in the upper-left corner of the screen.

Clear the Screen

Now, you will practice using the CLS command to clear the screen.

1. Make sure your computer is switched on and that the system has booted MS-DOS properly.

2. If your computer is not equipped with a hard disk drive, make sure the MS-DOS system disk (or a disk containing COMMAND.COM) is in drive A.

3. Type **cls** and press (Enter).

   The screen is cleared of any existing information, and the DOS prompt displays in the upper-left corner.

Using External Commands

External commands are program files that are not stored in memory. They are stored either on a hard disk or on a system disk that contains the MS-DOS program files. These are the files that use the COM and EXE extensions. Even though external commands are not resident in memory, they do, however, execute like internal commands. The user types the command—the program file's filename— at the DOS prompt and presses (Enter). As long as MS-DOS can find the program file, the program will be executed.

The important difference between the two types of MS-DOS commands is that external commands (files) must be read into memory before they can be executed; whereas, internal commands already exist in memory. To the user these processes happen very quickly, so the difference is not evident. You will practice using some DOS external commands later in this tutorial.

Preparing Diskettes

Although it is possible to buy diskettes already formatted and ready for use, it is far more common for new diskettes to be packaged completely blank or unformatted. To be able to use such diskettes, they must first be formatted in a personal computer.

Formatting is a dual-purpose disk-preparation process. First, the formatting process divides the disk's surface into sections called **sectors**. Sectors are areas that MS-DOS uses to store data. Second, the formatting process checks the disk for defective areas or bad spots. If any bad spots are detected, it is still possible to use the disk because the FORMAT command can structure the usable portions of the disk around the bad areas.

The FORMAT command reports the bad areas to you in the format report that displays on-screen following the formatting procedure. A typical format report is shown in Figure 1-4.

```
C:\>format b:
Insert new diskette for drive B:
and press ENTER when ready...

Checking existing disk format.
Formatting 1.44M
Format complete.

Volume label (11 characters, ENTER for none)? empty

   1457664 bytes total disk space
   1457664 bytes available on disk

       512 bytes in each allocation unit.
      2847 allocation units available on disk.

Volume Serial Number is 2430-16D7

Format another (Y/N)?
```

Figure 1-4

After the disk formatting procedure is complete, the FORMAT.COM program displays the format report. This format report shows that a 3.5-inch 1.44MB diskette was successfully formatted 100 percent.

Because the cost of disks is relatively inexpensive, it is best to discard any diskette that does not format 100 percent. An example of a format report showing bad areas on a newly formatted disk is shown in Figure 1-5.

Using the FORMAT Command

All personal computer users should be extremely careful with the FORMAT command. This external MS-DOS command will erase any data that exists on a diskette. Usually, the FORMAT command is used to prepare new diskettes; however, it can also be used to obliterate data intentionally from a used diskette so that no one can retrieve it. Make sure that you no longer need the data before you format a diskette that is not blank.

To use the FORMAT command, place a blank, unformatted disk (or one that contains data you are sure you no longer want) into a diskette drive. At the DOS prompt, type **FORMAT**, press (Spacebar), and then type the drive specification for the drive that contains the disk, as in this example:

```
format a:
```

```
C:\>format b:
Insert new diskette for drive B:
and press ENTER when ready...

Checking existing disk format.
Formatting 1.44M
Format complete.

Volume label (11 characters, ENTER for none)? empty

   1457664 bytes total disk space
     54680 bytes in bad sectors
   1402984 bytes available on disk

       512 bytes in each allocation unit.
      2847 allocation units available on disk.

Volume Serial Number is 2430-16D7

Format another (Y/N)?
```

Figure 1-5

This format report shows that the 3.5-inch 1.44MB diskette in drive B has some bad sectors. The diskette should be discarded because valuable data saved on it could be lost or adversely affected.

Figure 1-6

The FORMAT.COM program displays this message when you attempt to format a diskette with a capacity and recording density that does not match that of the specified drive.

```
C:\>format a:
Insert new diskette for drive A:
and press ENTER when ready...

Checking existing disk format.
Existing format differs from that specified.
This disk cannot be unformatted.
Proceed with Format (Y/N)?
```

When you press Enter, the program displays the following message:

```
Checking existing format
```

If the diskette to be formatted is the proper capacity for the specified disk drive, then the formatting process begins. A counter marking the percentage of disk space formatted appears below the "Checking existing format" message. When the formatting is complete, a message prompt displays asking whether you want to assign a volume label to the disk. A **volume label** is a name using from one to eleven characters that you can assign to the diskette. Press Enter if you do not want to assign a volume label to the diskette.

It is possible to format double-density 5.25-inch diskettes (360KB) in a high-density (1.2MB) disk drive or double-density 3.5-inch diskettes (720KB) in a high-density (1.44MB or 2.88MB) disk drive. To format double-density disks in disk drives that are capable of reading high-density disks, you must include a parameter that specifies the appropriate format. A **parameter** is the additional information MS-DOS needs to carry out the procedure specified in a particular program file. So, if, for example, you want to format a double-density 3.5-inch diskette (720KB) in disk drive B, which is capable of reading high-density 3.5-inch (1.44MB or 2.88MB) disks, then you must enter this command:

```
format b:/f:720
```

The program will check the capacity of the disk in the specified drive to make sure that it matches the format you specify in the command. If it does, the formatting process begins and proceeds as just described. If, however, there is a mismatch between the diskette's capacity and the capacity you specify, then a message similar to the one shown in Figure 1-6 appears. In this case DOS gives you the option of proceeding with the formatting procedure or canceling it.

Format a Diskette

Now, you will practice using the FORMAT command to format a blank diskette. Follow the directions that conform to your system's disk configuration.

Hard Disk Drive Systems:

1. Make sure your computer is switched on and that the system has booted DOS properly.

2. Insert a blank, unformatted diskette into drive A. Be sure the diskette's capacity matches the format capacity of the hard disk drive.

3. Type **format a:** and press Enter.

   A message appears indicating that the program is checking the diskette in drive A to verify that its capacity matches the format capacity specified in the command.

If the match is verified, the formatting process begins, and a counter displays showing the amount of disk space that has completed formatting. If the diskette's format does not match the command's specification, then the message shown in Figure 1-7 appears.

4. If the diskette's format does not match, type **n** to select the No response and cancel the format operation. If the proper disk is being formatted, wait for the formatting process to complete, then go to step 6.

5. If the disk you want to format is a 5.25-inch diskette, type **format a:/f:360** and press Enter. If you want to format a 3.5-inch disk, type **format a:/f:720** and press Enter.

   A message appears indicating that the program is checking the diskette in drive A to verify that it matches the specified format.

If the match is verified, the formatting process begins, and a counter appears showing the amount of disk space that has completed formatting.

When the formatting process has completed, a prompt appears asking whether you want to format another diskette.

6. Type **n** to select the No response.

   The formatting procedure is complete, and the DOS prompt appears.

7. Type **cls** to clear the screen.

```
C:\>format a:
Insert new diskette for drive A:
and press ENTER when ready...

Checking existing disk format.
Existing format differs from that specified.
This disk cannot be unformatted.
Proceed with Format (Y/N)?
```

Figure 1-7

If the FORMAT.COM program displays this message when you try to format a blank diskette, type **n** and press Enter to cancel the disk formatting procedure.

Diskette Drive Systems:

1. Make sure your computer is switched on and that the system has booted DOS properly.

2. Make sure that the system disk is in drive A and that drive A is the current drive.

3. Insert a blank, unformatted diskette into drive B. Be sure that the disk's capacity matches the format capacity of diskette drive B.

4. Type **format b:** and press [Enter].

   A message displays telling you to insert a blank diskette in the specified drive.

5. Make sure that the blank diskette is in drive B and press [Enter].

   A message appears indicating that the program is checking the diskette in drive B to verify that it matches the specified format.

If the match can be verified, the formatting process begins, and a counter appears showing the amount of disk space that has completed formatting.

Once formatting has been completed, a prompt appears asking whether you want to format another diskette.

6. Type **n** to select the No response.

   The formatting procedure is complete, and the DOS prompt appears.

7. Type **cls** to clear the screen.

Managing Files and Disk Space

Both hard disks and diskettes are akin to filing cabinets, which hold folders that, in turn, hold paper documents. Similarly, electronic files stored on a disk are very much like electronic file folders because they store related sets of data, such as word processed documents, spreadsheet calculations, programming instructions, or other kinds of data. And, just as a filing cabinet contains drawers so that the file folders can be organized, MS-DOS lets you create directories that serve as file drawers for organizing related sets of files. A **directory** is a special file that MS-DOS stores on disk in the same way it stores any file; a directory, however, is used primarily to group a set of files that are related in some meaningful way to the user.

Storing Files in Directories

There are two types of directories for disks in the MS-DOS environment. The **root directory** is the main directory that establishes the total amount of disk space available for storing files on the disk. All disks have a root directory. In addition to files, the root directory can hold the other type of directory, which is often referred to as a **subdirectory**. (Note that the terms *directory* and *subdirectory* are often used interchangeably.)

The user creates subdirectories to group files that are related in some meaningful way to the user. Subdirectories serve as filing cabinet drawers by organizing files that are stored on disk into groups. All the files in *any* directory must have unique file names; no two

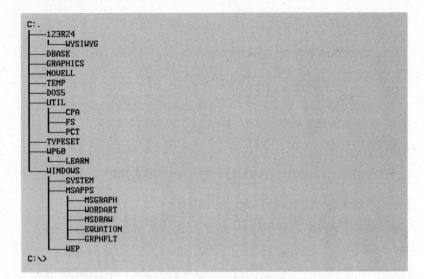

```
C:.
    ├──123R24
    │   └──WYSIWYG
    ├──DBASE
    ├──GRAPHICS
    ├──NOUELL
    ├──TEMP
    ├──DOS5
    ├──UTIL
    │       ├──CPA
    │       ├──FS
    │       └──PCT
    ├──TYPESET
    ├──WP60
    │   └──LEARN
    └──WINDOWS
            ├──SYSTEM
            ├──MSAPPS
            │       ├──MSGRAPH
            │       ├──WORDART
            │       ├──MSDRAW
            │       ├──EQUATION
            │       └──GRPHFLT
            └──WEP
C:\>
```

Figure 1-8

This is an example of a directory tree structure, or the filing system, for a hard disk.

files within any directory can have the exact same file name. You can, however, store multiple files with the same file name on the same disk, as long as each file is stored within a different subdirectory.

Like root directories, directories can store subdirectories. Strictly speaking, though, any directory created by the user is a subdirectory that branches from the root directory or from other subdirectories. The term **branch** refers to the hierarchical structure, or tree structure, that is characteristic of the directory system on any disk. An example of this directory tree structure is shown in Figure 1-8. For any subdirectory, the directory (root directory or subdirectory) in which it resides is known as its **parent directory**.

The size of any subdirectory (as well as the number of files stored within it) is limited to the amount of available disk space. So, while the root directory always has a fixed size, subdirectories, like files, vary in size. And, although *all* disks have root directories, they do not necessarily have to have subdirectories.

Subdirectories are set up by the user to organize files; they are recommended for use on hard disks, which have much more storage space than diskettes. Subdirectories can be created on diskettes, but their limited storage capacity makes the use of subdirectories less practical than on hard disks.

Creating a Subdirectory

You create subdirectories with the DOS MKDIR command, which you can shorten to MD when you type the command at the DOS prompt. The MKDIR command, short for "make directory," is one of the internal DOS commands carried out by COMMAND.COM, so it is always available because it resides in memory after the computer has booted DOS. To use the command you must include the name of the subdirectory that you want to create. For example, suppose you want to create a subdirectory named NOTES in the root directory on a hard disk. At the DOS prompt, type the command as follows:

md\notes

When you press [Enter], the subdirectory is created and stored in the root directory on the disk in the current disk drive. Alternatively, you can substitute a space for the backslash (\) when you type this command, as in this example:

```
md notes
```

The distinction between using the backslash and using a space in the command will be made clear in the next section, which explains how to change the current subdirectory.

Names for subdirectories are governed by the same rules that apply to file names. Subdirectory names can have extensions as well. For example, you can create a subdirectory named DOCUMENT.JAN.

Create Subdirectories

Now, you will practice using the internal DOS command MD to create a subdirectory on the diskette you have just formatted. In the instructions that follow, substitute drive B for drive A if your system is not equipped with a hard disk drive.

1. Make sure your computer is switched on and that the system has booted MS-DOS properly.

2. Insert a formatted diskette in drive A (or drive B), if necessary.

3. If drive C is the current drive, type **a:** and press [Enter]. If drive A is the current drive, type **b:** and press [Enter].

   The specified drive is now current.

4. Type **md\subdir.1** and press [Enter].

   A subdirectory named SUBDIR.1 is created within the current disk's root directory.

5. Type **md\subdir.1\subdir.1a** and press [Enter].

   A subdirectory named SUBDIR.1A is created within its parent directory SUBDIR.1.

Changing the Current Subdirectory

Notice that when you create a subdirectory, its parent directory, which was current when you entered the MD command, remains current after the subdirectory is created. MS-DOS provides another internal command, the CHDIR command, that lets you change the current subdirectory as easily as you can change the current disk drive. The CHDIR command is short for "change directory," and you can shorten it to CD when you type it at the DOS prompt. Using the previous example, suppose you want to make the subdirectory NOTES the current subdirectory. The command you type at the DOS prompt is this:

```
cd\notes
```

When you press [Enter], the specified subdirectory becomes the current directory. The DOS prompt then indicates the current directory, as follows:

```
C:\NOTES>
```

```
C:\NOTES\RESEARCH>cd notes
Invalid directory

C:\NOTES\RESEARCH>cd\notes

C:\NOTES>
```

Figure 1-9

Because a backslash (\) was not used with the first CD command, it tells DOS to change the current directory to a subdirectory named NOTES, which doesn't exist in the current directory, RESEARCH. The second CD command works because the backslash correctly tells DOS that the subdirectory NOTES is in the disk's root directory.

As with the MD command, MS-DOS will permit you to substitute a space for the backslash (\) when the parent directory containing the subdirectory you want to make current is the current directory. Be aware that substituting a space for a backslash in the MD and CD commands works only when the specified subdirectory's parent directory is current. To MS-DOS the first backslash in any command refers to a disk's root directory. If a space is substituted for the backslash, then MS-DOS assumes the subdirectory specified in the command resides in the current directory, whether it's the root directory or any other subdirectory.

To illustrate, suppose the subdirectory NOTES contains a subdirectory named RESEARCH, which is the current directory. To change the current directory to its parent directory—that is, to change the current directory from RESEARCH to NOTES—the backslash *must* be used in the CD command to tell MS-DOS that the subdirectory NOTES resides in the root directory. Figure 1-9 shows two attempts at changing the current subdirectory to NOTES. The first attempt is unsuccessful because it tells MS-DOS to make the subdirectory NOTES within the subdirectory RESEARCH current. The message "Invalid directory" indicates that the current subdirectory (RESEARCH) does not contain the subdirectory NOTES. The second attempt is successful because the backslash tells MS-DOS to change the current directory to NOTES in the root directory.

Returning to the Root Directory

No matter which subdirectory is current within the current disk's directory system, you can always return to the root directory using the CD command. Simply enter the CD command followed by a backslash (\) to return to the root directory from any subdirectory branch. For example, suppose the RESEARCH subdirectory within the NOTES subdirectory is current and you want to return directly to the root directory. First you enter the command at the DOS prompt as follows:

cd \

Then, when you press Enter, the current disk's root directory becomes the current directory.

Backing out of Subdirectory Branches

DOS also lets you back out of subdirectories, one by one, by using the CD command and two periods to change the current subdirectory to its parent subdirectory, as follows:

```
cd..
```

When you press Enter, the parent directory for the subdirectory that was just current becomes current. Because this command requires only five keystrokes, it is often quicker for switching current directories because you don't have to type the name for the parent directory.

Change the Current Subdirectory

Now, you will practice using the internal DOS command CD to change the current directory.

1. Make sure your computer is switched on and that the system has booted DOS properly.

2. Make sure the diskette on which you created subdirectories in the last exercise is in drive A (or drive B if your computer does not have a hard disk drive).

3. If necessary, make disk drive A current (or make disk drive B current if your computer does not have a hard disk drive).

4. Type **cd subdir.1** and press Enter.

   The specified subdirectory is current.

5. Type **cd subdir.1a** and press Enter.

   The specified subdirectory is current, as shown in Figure 1-10.

6. Type **cd..** and press Enter.

   Subdirectory SUBDIR.1, the parent directory for SUBDIR.1A, is now current.

Figure 1-10

After making the subdirectory SUBDIR.1A current in step 5, your screen should look like this.

```
C:\>a:
A:\>md\subdir.1
A:\>md\subdir.1\subdir.1a
A:\>cd subdir.1
A:\SUBDIR.1>cd subdir.1a
A:\SUBDIR.1\SUBDIR.1A>
```

7. Type **cd..** and press Enter.

   The root directory for the current disk is now current.

8. Type **cd subdir.1\subdir.1a** and press Enter.

   The subdirectory SUBDIR.1A is current.

9. Type **cd** and press Enter.

   The root directory for the current disk is current.

Using Paths and File Specifications

When you enter subdirectory names and file names with DOS commands, you are providing DOS with a path to a specific file. A **path** is the course that travels from the root directory of the specified drive, through any subdirectories, to a file specification. A **path name** is the description that MS-DOS can interpret to locate a file. When MS-DOS must locate a particular file you want, it looks for the file's full name or file specification. Recall that a file specification is the file's complete file name, including the filename and extension (for example, LETTER.DOC). For MS-DOS to know where to find a particular file, it searches the disk that contains the file through a specific path. For example, suppose you want MS-DOS to locate a file named LIBRARY.TXT, which is stored in the subdirectory RESEARCH. The full path name and file specification for this file is as follows:

```
C:\NOTES\RESEARCH\LIBRARY.TXT
```

As you become a proficient user of personal computers and DOS, you will find that path names are extremely important. They can be used to establish where in a disk's directory system you want MS-DOS and your applications programs to work.

Listing Files with the DIR Command

The ability to see the contents of a disk or subdirectory on screen is vital to file organization tasks. DOS provides an internal command, the DIR command, that lets you do just that. Of course, DIR is short for "directory." When you type DIR at the DOS prompt and press Enter, all file names and subdirectory names in the current directory appear on screen, as shown in Figure 1-11.

Just as there is always a default, or current, disk drive, there is also always a default, or current, directory. After a personal computer boots MS-DOS, the current directory is generally the root directory of the disk that stores the MS-DOS files. As mentioned previously, the single backslash (\) that follows the colon in the DOS prompt's drive specification (for example, C:\) indicates that the root directory is the current directory on the current disk.

The DIR command is a very useful and important command because it provides a lot more information than just the names of files and subdirectories. It also provides the sizes of files, in bytes; the files' creation dates and times; the amount of current disk space that the files and subdirectories occupy; and the amount of free, or available, disk space on the current disk, in addition to other information.

Figure 1-11

This is an example of the information that appears when you issue the DIR command for the current directory. DOS displays information about the current disk: names, sizes, and creation dates and times for subdirectories and files stored in the current directory; and the amount of available space left on the current disk.

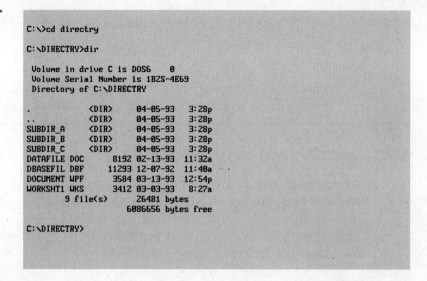

```
C:\>cd directory

C:\DIRECTRY>dir

 Volume in drive C is DOS6    0
 Volume Serial Number is 1B2S-4E69
 Directory of C:\DIRECTRY

.             <DIR>      04-05-93    3:28p
..            <DIR>      04-05-93    3:28p
SUBDIR_A      <DIR>      04-05-93    3:28p
SUBDIR_B      <DIR>      04-05-93    3:28p
SUBDIR_C      <DIR>      04-05-93    3:28p
DATAFILE DOC       8192  02-13-93   11:32a
DBASEFIL DBF      11293  12-07-92   11:40a
DOCUMENT WPF       3584  03-13-93   12:54p
WORKSHT1 WKS       3412  03-03-93    8:27a
        9 file(s)        26481 bytes
                      6086656 bytes free

C:\DIRECTRY>
```

Display a Directory List

You will practice using the internal DOS command DIR to list files in the current directory on the current disk.

Displaying a Directory List on Hard Disk Drive Systems:

1. Make sure your computer is switched on and that the system has booted DOS properly.

2. If necessary, insert the diskette that you formatted earlier into drive A.

3. If necessary, type **c:** and press [Enter] to make the hard disk drive current.

4. Type **dir** and press [Enter].

   A list of all the files and subdirectories stored in the root directory on the hard disk appears. Depending on the number of files and subdirectories, some of the information may scroll off screen.

5. Type **a:** and press [Enter].

6. Type **dir** and press [Enter].

   A directory list for the root directory of the current disk in drive A appears. Notice that only the subdirectory you created earlier is listed.

7. Type **c:** and press [Enter].

Displaying a Directory List on Diskette Drive Systems:

1. Make sure your computer is switched on and that the system has booted DOS properly.

2. If necessary, insert the diskette that contains the subdirectories you created earlier into drive B.

3. If necessary, type **a:** and press Enter to make disk drive A, which contains the MS-DOS system disk, current.

4. Type **dir** and press Enter.

   A list of all the MS-DOS program files stored in the system disk's root directory appears. Depending on the number of files, some of the information may scroll off screen.

Using Parameters with the DIR Command

As you have just seen, information scrolls very quickly from the bottom to the top of the screen when you enter the DIR command by itself. This makes it virtually impossible to read the information that scrolls off screen. DOS provides two parameters that you can include with the DIR command, either separately or together, which make it possible to read all of the directory listing information.

Using the /p Option

You may use the /p option—the "p" stands for "pause"—with the DIR command to pause scrolling momentarily when enough information for one screen displays, as shown in Figure 1-12. The format for the command is as follows:

`dir/p`

Notice in Figure 1-12 that the following message, or prompt, displays at the bottom of the screen:

`Press any key to continue . . .`

When you are through reading the partial directory list, press any key (Spacebar is usually most convenient) and the next screen of information will scroll into view. The same message prompt appears if there is additional information that will not fit on one screen. Continue pressing any key to scroll the list until a DOS prompt appears.

```
Volume in drive C is DOS6    0
Volume Serial Number is 1B2S-4E69
Directory of C:\DOS6

.              <DIR>      04-08-92    4:41p
..             <DIR>      04-08-92    4:41p
4201     CPI      6404 04-09-91    5:00a
4208     CPI       720 04-09-91    5:00a
5202     CPI       395 04-09-91    5:00a
ANSI     SYS      9065 02-12-93    6:00a
APPEND   EXE     10774 02-12-93    6:00a
APPNOTES TXT      9701 04-09-91    5:00a
ASSIGN   COM      6399 04-09-91    5:00a
ATTRIB   EXE     11165 02-12-93    6:00a
BACKUP   EXE     36092 04-09-91    5:00a
CHKDSK   EXE     12908 02-12-93    6:00a
CHKLIST  CPS       108 04-14-92    9:21a
CHKSTATE SYS     41600 02-12-93    6:00a
CHOICE   COM      1754 02-12-93    6:00a
COMMAND  COM     52925 02-12-93    6:00a
COMP     EXE     14282 04-09-91    5:00a
COUNTRY  SYS     17066 02-12-93    6:00a
DBLSPACE BIN     50284 02-12-93    6:00a
Press any key to continue . . .
```

Figure 1-12

When included with the DIR command, the /p option pauses the scrolling of the directory list so that you can read the information before displaying the rest of the list.

Figure 1-13

When included with the DIR command, the /w option displays the list of file names and subdirectories for the current disk and directory across the width of the screen. Notice that other information about the files and sub-directories, such as sizes and creation dates, does not display.

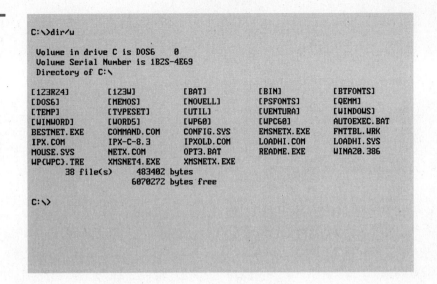

```
C:\>dir/w

 Volume in drive C is DOS6    0
 Volume Serial Number is 1B2S-4E69
 Directory of C:\

[123R24]        [123W]          [BAT]          [BIN]          [BTFONTS]
[DOS6]          [MEMOS]         [NOVELL]       [PSFONTS]      [QEMM]
[TEMP]          [TYPESET]       [UTIL]         [VENTURA]      [WINDOWS]
[WINWORD]       [WORD5]         [WP60]         [WPC60]        AUTOEXEC.BAT
BESTNET.EXE     COMMAND.COM     CONFIG.SYS     EMSNETX.EXE    FNTTBL.WRK
IPX.COM         IPX-C-8.3       IPXOLD.COM     LOADHI.COM     LOADHI.SYS
MOUSE.SYS       NETX.COM        OPT3.BAT       README.EXE     WINA20.386
WP(WPC).TRE     XMSNET4.EXE     XMSNETX.EXE
          38 file(s)      483402 bytes
                         6070272 bytes free

C:\>
```

Using the /w Option

Including the /w option—the "w" stands for "wide"—with the DIR command causes the file names and subdirectories to display across the width of the screen. The format for the command is as follows:

```
                              dir/w
```

This lets you display more items in the current directory than display when the DIR command alone (or with the /p option) lists the information in a single column. The list that appears when you use the /w option, however, does not include file size or creation date and times. Only the names for files and subdirectories appear, as shown in Figure 1-13. Notice that subdirectory names are enclosed in square brackets.

You may also use the /w and /p options together when the current directory contains more items than can be displayed on screen with the /w option alone.

Use DIR Command Options

Now, you will practice using the /p and /w options with the DIR command.

Hard Disk Drive Systems:

1. Make sure your computer is switched on and that the system has booted DOS properly.

2. Make sure the diskette on which you created subdirectories earlier is in drive A.

3. Type **c:** to make the hard disk drive current, if necessary.

4. Type **dir/w** and press (Enter).

   All files and subdirectories in the hard disk's root directory display across the width of the screen.

5. Type **cd\dos60** and press (Enter).

```
Volume in drive C is DOS6    0
Volume Serial Number is 1B2S-4E69
Directory of C:\DOS6

.            <DIR>      04-08-92    4:41p
..           <DIR>      04-08-92    4:41p
4201     CPI       6404 04-09-91    5:00a
4208     CPI        720 04-09-91    5:00a
5202     CPI        395 04-09-91    5:00a
ANSI     SYS       9065 02-12-93    6:00a
APPEND   EXE      10774 02-12-93    6:00a
APPNOTES TXT       9701 04-09-91    5:00a
ASSIGN   COM       6399 04-09-91    5:00a
ATTRIB   EXE      11165 02-12-93    6:00a
BACKUP   EXE      36092 04-09-91    5:00a
CHKDSK   EXE      12908 02-12-93    6:00a
CHKLIST  CPS        108 04-14-92    9:21a
CHKSTATE SYS      41600 02-12-93    6:00a
CHOICE   COM       1754 02-12-93    6:00a
COMMAND  COM      52925 02-12-93    6:00a
COMP     EXE      14282 04-09-91    5:00a
COUNTRY  SYS      17066 02-12-93    6:00a
DBLSPACE BIN      50284 02-12-93    6:00a
Press any key to continue . . .
```

Figure 1-14

After entering the DIR command with the /p option in step 6, a directory list similar to this should appear.

The subdirectory containing DOS program files is current.

(*Note*: If you are using another version of DOS, or the DOS program files are stored in a subdirectory with another name, type that name instead for step 5.)

6. Type **dir/p** and press Enter.

   A partial list of files in the DOS6 subdirectory displays, as shown in Figure 1-14.

7. Press Spacebar (or any other key) to scroll the directory list.

8. Press Spacebar (or any other key) as many times as necessary to scroll the entire directory list.

9. Type **dir/p/w** and press Enter.

   A partial list of files in the DOS6 subdirectory displays across the width of the screen.

10. Press Spacebar (or any other key) to complete the command.

Diskette Drive Systems:

1. Make sure your computer is switched on and that the system has booted DOS properly.

2. Make sure the DOS system disk is in drive A and that the diskette on which you created subdirectories earlier is in drive B.

3. Type **a:** to make diskette drive A current, if necessary.

4. Type **dir/w** and press Enter.

   All MS-DOS program files display across the width of the screen.

5. Type **dir/p** and press Enter.

   A partial list of the MS-DOS program files displays.

6. Press (Spacebar) (or any other key) to scroll the directory list.

   More of the list of MS-DOS program files display.

7. Press (Spacebar) (or any other key) as many times as is necessary to complete the command.

Using Wild Card Characters

With several DOS commands it is often useful to perform operations on selected files. DOS **wild card** characters can be included in command line file specifications to indicate several files in a specific disk location for an operation. For instance, you can use wild card characters in a file specification with the DIR command to list a specific group of files in a subdirectory. This allows you to search a subdirectory for selected files without having to display all the file names stored in the subdirectory.

DOS provides two wild card characters: the asterisk (*) and the question mark (?). The **asterisk** (*) is used to represent any string of consecutive characters in a file name's filename or extension. For example, the file specification *.* represents all files in a specific subdirectory. The file specification *.DOC refers to all files in a subdirectory that have the file name extension DOC.

The **question mark** (?) is used to represent any single character in a filename or extension. For instance, the file specification BUDGET9?.WK1 refers to all files in a subdirectory with filenames that begin with the character string "BUDGET9," followed by any single character, and have the extension "WK1."

You can also combine wild card characters in a file specification. For example, the file specification BUDGET9?.* included with the DIR command would list all files beginning with "BUDGET9" followed by any single character and any extension.

Use Wild Card Characters with the DIR Command

You will use the asterisk (*) and question mark (?) wild card characters with the DIR command.

Hard Disk Drive Systems:

1. Make sure your computer is switched on and that the system has booted DOS properly.

2. Make sure the diskette on which you created subdirectories earlier is in drive A.

3. Make the subdirectory containing the DOS program files current, if necessary.

4. Type **dir *.exe /p** and press (Enter).

   The first several files with the EXE extension appear.

5. Press (Spacebar) (or any other key) to scroll the list.

6. Press $\boxed{\text{Spacebar}}$ (or any other key) as many times as is necessary to complete the command.

7. Type **dir dos*.*** and press $\boxed{\text{Enter}}$.

   All file names in the current directory that begin with the characters "DOS" appear.

8. Type **dir dos???.*** and press $\boxed{\text{Enter}}$.

   One file name, DOSKEY.COM, appears because this is the only file name in the current directory that begins with the characters "DOS" and is followed by three characters only, as specified in the command.

Diskette Drive Systems:

1. Make sure your computer is switched on and that the system has booted DOS properly.

2. Make sure the DOS system disk is in drive A and the diskette on which you created subdirectories earlier is in drive B.

3. Type **a:** to make diskette drive A current, if necessary.

4. Type **dir *.exe /p** and press $\boxed{\text{Enter}}$.

   The first several files with the EXE extension appear.

5. Press $\boxed{\text{Spacebar}}$ (or any other key) to scroll the list.

6. Press $\boxed{\text{Spacebar}}$ (or any other key) as many times as is necessary to complete the command.

7. Type **dir dos*.*** and press $\boxed{\text{Enter}}$.

   All file names in the current directory that begin with the characters "DOS" appear.

8. Type **dir dos???.*** and press $\boxed{\text{Enter}}$.

   One file name, DOSKEY.COM, appears because this is the only file name in the current directory that begins with the characters "DOS" and is followed by three characters only, as specified in the command.

Removing Subdirectories

DOS makes it very easy to delete subdirectories you no longer want stored on a disk. You do this with the RMDIR command, which is short for "remove directory." You can shorten the RMDIR command to RD when you type it at the DOS prompt. To remove a subdirectory, use the following procedure:

- Make sure the subdirectory you want to remove is empty, that is, it does not contain any files or subdirectories.

- Change the current directory to any subdirectory that is not the subdirectory you want to remove.

- Type the RD command, followed by the exact path to the subdirectory you want to delete, and press $\boxed{\text{Enter}}$.

For example, suppose you want to delete the subdirectory RESEARCH, which is the current subdirectory. First, you must make sure the subdirectory contains no data or program files and no subdirectories. You will learn how to do this in the next lesson. Next, change the current directory to its parent directory, NOTES. Finally, enter the following at the DOS prompt:

```
rd\notes\research
```

Because the parent directory is the current directory, you can also enter the following command to achieve the same result:

```
rd research
```

Removing Subdirectories

Now, you will practice using the internal RD command to delete the subdirectories that you have created on your diskette.

1. Make sure your computer is switched on and that the system has booted DOS properly.

2. Make sure the diskette on which you created subdirectories is in drive A (or in drive B if your computer does not have a hard disk drive).

3. If necessary, make sure that drive A is current (or drive B if your computer does not have a hard disk drive).

4. Type **cd\subdir.1\subdir.1a** and press Enter.

   Subdirectory SUBDIR.1A in SUBDIR.1 is current.

5. Type **dir** and press Enter.

   A message displays telling you there are no files in the current subdirectory.

6. Type **cd..** and press Enter.

   Subdirectory SUBDIR.1A's parent directory, SUBDIR.1, is now current.

7. Type **rd subdir.1a** and press Enter.

   Subdirectory SUBDIR.1A is deleted from the current disk.

8. Type **dir** and press Enter.

   A message displays telling you there are no files in the current subdirectory.

9. Type **cd** and press Enter.

   The current disk's root directory is current.

10. Type **rd\subdir.1** and press Enter.

    Subdirectory SUBDIR.1 is deleted from the current disk.

Command Summary

Internal Commands

CLS	Clears the screen of information and displays a single DOS prompt in the upper-left corner
DIR	Displays a listing of files, subdirectories, and other disk information for the current or specified disk and/or directory
MKDIR (MD)	Creates a subdirectory
CHDIR (CD)	Changes the current, or default, subdirectory
RMDIR (RD)	Removes, or deletes, a subdirectory

External Commands

FORMAT.COM	Formats a diskette so it can be used to store data

Review Questions

1. Describe generally what occurs during the booting process.

2. Which keys do you press to reload MS-DOS (perform a warm boot)? Describe how you press them.

3. Which keys can you use to correct typing mistakes before entering a command?

4. Describe the process that occurs when you issue the MS-DOS FORMAT command to format a new, blank diskette.

5. Given the following DOS prompt and command, describe the result of the operation that will occur when ⌊Enter⌋ is pressed to enter the command.

```
C:/>md\public
```

Application Projects

1. Perform a cold boot. If the personal computer with which you are working is already switched on and a DOS prompt displays, switch the computer off and wait approximately 60 seconds. Then perform a cold boot. After MS-DOS has booted, perform a warm boot.

2. Format a blank diskette, and then do the following:

   a. Create the subdirectories DOCUMNTS, WORKSHTS, and DBFILES in the diskette's root directory.

   b. Display a directory listing for the diskette's root directory. What information does the directory listing tell you? How much available file storage space is on the disk currently? How much disk space do the three directories occupy?

   c. Remove the three subdirectories from the diskette.

Figure 1-15

For Application Project 3, describe the reasons why the five commands shown here did not work, as well as how they can be corrected so that they do work.

```
C:\>cd..
Invalid directory

C:\>cd directry\subdir_a\
Invalid directory

C:\>date 12-7-79

Invalid date
Enter new date (mm-dd-yy): ^C

C:\>md *special
Unable to create directory

C:\>a:


Not ready reading drive A
Abort, Retry, Fail?


C:\>a
Bad command or file name
```

3. Figure 1-15 shows five commands that were not entered correctly. Describe the problem that caused MS-DOS to return the error messages shown for each command. How can each command be corrected to work properly?

4. Describe exactly what will occur when the following commands are entered at the following DOS prompts.

   a. C:\>format a:

   b. C:\PROJECTS>md budgets\first_q

   c. A:\>dir b:\

   d. C:\PROJECTS\BUDGETS>a:

   e. C:\DOCUMNTS>rd\projects\budgets

   f. C:\DOS60>dir f*.com

   g. C:\>dir \dos60\m????.*

LESSON 2   MANAGING FILES WITH DOS

Objectives

After completing this lesson, you will be able to do the following:

- Use the internal DOS command COPY to copy one or more files.
- Use the external DOS command MOVE (MS-DOS 6.0) to move one or more files and/or create a directory.
- Use the internal DOS command REN to change the name of one or more files.
- Use the internal DOS command DEL (or ERASE) to delete one or more files from a disk.
- Use the internal DOS command TYPE to display the content of a text file on screen.
- Use the external DOS command PRINT to send data stored in a text file to a printer.
- Use the external CHKDSK command to check the current status of a disk.
- Load, use, and exit the MS-DOS Shell program for an alternative interface to the text mode command line.

Using the COPY Command

The internal DOS command COPY is used to make duplicate data files, which can be stored in the same disk locations as the original files, in different directories on the same disk, or on different disks. The COPY command is one of the most frequently used DOS commands, and it is extremely useful for managing files and backing up valuable data.

When you enter the COPY command, DOS copies the data stored in the file you are copying, called the source file, to another file, called the target file. The source and target file names can be the same as long as the files are not stored in the same subdirectory. When you enter the COPY command, DOS must be able to locate the source file; otherwise, the message "File not found" displays when you try to execute the command.

On the other hand, DOS will *not* inform you that a target file name already exists if you specify an existing file name for storing the copied data. Instead, DOS overwrites the existing data with the new data in the source file. Be very careful with this COPY command feature. It can be useful if you intend to replace the existing version of a file with updated information. However, you can lose valuable data if you do not want the existing data to be replaced.

Copying a File to Another Disk

The COPY command is well suited for creating a backup copy of an original file. For example, suppose you want to copy the file BUDGET.WK1 from the hard disk's root directory to a diskette. You would enter the command as follows:

```
copy c:\budget.wk1 a:
```

When you press Enter, DOS copies the data stored in the source file BUDGET.WK1 from the root directory on disk drive C to a diskette in disk drive A. Like the source file, the duplicate version on the diskette in drive A is stored in a file named BUDGET.WK1.

You can copy data to a different target file name by specifying a new name with the COPY command. For example, suppose you want to copy the same data to the diskette, only this time assign a new name to the target file. You would enter the command at the DOS prompt as follows:

```
copy c:\budget.wk1 a:\budget2.wk1
```

In this case, the target file has a different file name than the original file but stores the same data.

It is also possible to copy a file from another disk to the current disk. In this case, you do not have to specify the target disk location when you enter the COPY command, as long as you want the target file to have the same file name as the source file. For example, suppose you want to copy a file named ADDRESS.DAT to the current hard disk subdirectory from a diskette in drive B. You can enter the COPY command for this operation as follows:

```
copy b:\address.dat
```

When you press Enter to execute this command, DOS copies the data in the source file ADDRESS.DAT on the diskette in drive B to a target file with the same name in the current subdirectory.

Copying a File to the Same Disk

You can store copies of original files on the same disk, either in the same subdirectory or in another subdirectory. Of course, files storing duplicate data in the same subdirectory must have different file names. When you want to store copies of files in other directories on the same disk, simply specify the source and target paths with the COPY command, as shown in this example:

```
copy \proposal\bid.txt \budgets
```

Here, DOS copies the data stored in the file BID.TXT from the subdirectory PROPOSAL to the subdirectory BUDGETS, and the target file has the same file name as the source file. If a file is copied to the same subdirectory, then the target file must have a different file name, as demonstrated in this following example:

```
copy \proposal\bid.txt newbid.txt
```

Copying Several Files

In Lesson 1 you were introduced briefly to wild card characters and their use with the DIR command for listing specific sets of files. Wild card characters also can be used with the COPY command to copy multiple files from one disk location to another.

Copy Files

You will use the COPY command to copy selected files to different disk locations.

Hard Disk Drive Systems:

1. Make sure your computer is switched on and that the system has booted DOS properly.
2. Make sure the diskette you formatted and used for Lesson 1's exercises is inserted in disk drive A (or drive B).
3. If necessary, make drive C the current disk drive.
4. Type **cd dos60** and press (Enter).

(*Note*: If your DOS program files are stored in a subdirectory with another name, type that name, instead, for step 4.)

5. Type **copy readme.txt a:** and press (Enter).

(*Note*: If your diskette is in a drive other than drive A, enter the appropriate drive specification in place of a:\.)

The file named README.TXT stored in the DOS directory on the hard disk copies to the diskette in drive A (or drive B).

6. Type **a:** (or the drive specification for the drive that contains your diskette) and press (Enter).
7. Type **dir** and press (Enter).

The directory list shows the file you copied from your hard disk.

8. Type **copy readme.txt datacopy.fil** and press (Enter).

The contents stored in the file named README.TXT are copied to another file in the same directory named DATACOPY.FIL.

9. Type **dir** and press (Enter).

The directory list shows the two files. Notice that they are identical in size and have the same creation dates and times.

10. Type **md\practice** and press (Enter).

The subdirectory PRACTICE is created in the root directory on your work diskette.

11. Type **cd\practice** and press (Enter).

The subdirectory PRACTICE is current.

Figure 2-1

Your directory list should look like this after you copy the two files in the diskette's root directory to the subdirectory named PRACTICE on the same diskette.

```
        2 file(s)      123714 bytes
                       237568 bytes free

A:\>md\practice

A:\>cd\practice

A:\PRACTICE>copy a:\*.* *.bak
A:\README.TXT
A:\DATACOPY.FIL
        2 file(s) copied

A:\PRACTICE>dir

 Volume in drive A has no label
 Directory of A:\PRACTICE

.              <DIR>    10-27-93   4:12p
..             <DIR>    10-27-93   4:12p
DATACOPY BAK    61857 03-10-93   6:00a
README   BAK    61857 03-10-93   6:00a
        4 file(s)      123714 bytes
                       111616 bytes free

A:\PRACTICE>
```

12. Type **copy a:*.* *.bak** and press Enter.

    The two files in the root directory on the diskette copy to the subdirectory PRACTICE. Both copies are named with the extension BAK.

13. Type **dir** and press Enter.

    The directory list shows the contents of the current directory, as shown in Figure 2-1.

14. Type **copy c:\\dos60\\packing.lst** and press Enter.

    The file named PACKING.LST, stored in the DOS directory on disk drive C, copies to the current subdirectory PRACTICE on the current diskette.

15. Type **dir** and press Enter.

    Observe that the current directory contains three files you have copied.

16. Type **cls** and press Enter to clear the screen.

Diskette Drive Systems:

1. Make sure your computer is switched on and that the system has booted DOS properly.

2. Make sure the MS-DOS system disk is in drive A and that drive A is the current disk drive.

3. Insert the diskette you formatted and used in Lesson 1's exercises into drive B.

4. Type **dir** and press Enter.

    A directory list for the DOS system disk in drive A appears.

5. Look for a file name that has any extension besides COM, EXE, or SYS.

6. Copy the file to the diskette in drive B by typing **copy** and pressing Spacebar and then typing the file name followed by the drive specification **b:**. Then press Enter.

7. Type **b:** and press Enter to make your work diskette current.

8. Copy the file on the diskette to another file in the same directory named DATACOPY.FIL.

9. Do steps 9–13 from "Copying on Hard Disk Drive Systems" above.

Moving Files

The ability to move files between disks and/or directories with a single command is now available with the latest release of MS-DOS, version 6.0. If you are using this version of DOS, then you can move files with the external DOS command MOVE. If you are using an earlier version of DOS, this command is not available to you; however, you can use combinations of the COPY, DEL (or ERASE), and/or REN commands to achieve similar results.

Like the COPY command, the MOVE command requires a source path and a target path. Unlike the COPY command, the data in the source file is removed entirely from its original disk location when it is moved (in effect, copied) to the target disk location.

For example, if you want to move a single file named CHAPTER1.WPD from a hard disk subdirectory named BOOK to the root directory of a diskette in drive A, you would enter the MOVE command as follows:

```
move c:\book\chapter1.wpd a:\
```

When you press Enter to execute this command, DOS transfers the data stored in the subdirectory BOOK to the root directory of the diskette in drive A in a file named CHAPTER1.WPD. You can also move a file from one directory to another on the same disk.

Wild card characters can be used in file specifications for the MOVE command to move more than one file in a single operation. For example, suppose you want to move several document files to another disk or directory. You would enter the MOVE command as follows:

```
move c:\book\*.wpd a:\
```

When you press Enter to execute this command, DOS moves the data stored in each file with the WPD extension from the directory named BOOK to the diskette in drive A. If you want to move one or more files from the current directory, then you need only specify the target path with the MOVE command.

Renaming Files with the MOVE Command

You can also use the MOVE command to rename one or more files. Because DOS recognizes the entire path as part of the file's specification, you can specify a new file name or names along with the target path. For example, suppose you want to move and rename a file named INVENTRY.DBF from a hard disk subdirectory to a diskette's root directory. You would enter the MOVE command as follows:

```
move c:\data\inventry.dbf b:\inv_data.dbf
```

When you press Enter to execute this command, DOS moves the data stored in the source file to the new disk location, and stores the data in a file with the new name.

Creating a Directory with the MOVE Command

In addition to moving and/or renaming files, the MOVE command can be used to create a new directory that serves as the target disk location for the file or files you are moving. To do this, you specify a name for the subdirectory you want to create in the MOVE command's target path. For example, suppose you want to transfer data stored in several files from one hard disk subdirectory to another and create a new directory at the same time. You would enter the MOVE command as follows:

```
move c:\book\*.wpd c:\bookcopy\
```

When you press [Enter] to execute this command, the following prompt appears:

```
Make directory  c:\bookcopy ? [yn]
```

If you type **y** and press [Enter], DOS creates the new subdirectory and moves the data stored in the specified files to the new subdirectory, storing the data with the same file names.

Move Files and Create a New Directory

You will use the MOVE command to move files and create a new subdirectory on your working diskette.

(*Note*: If you are using an earlier version of DOS, you will not have access to the MOVE command. Skip this exercise and go to the next section, "Using the REN Command to Rename a File.")

1. Make sure your computer is switched on and that the system has booted DOS properly.

2. Make sure your work diskette is in drive A (or drive B).

3. If necessary, make the drive that contains your work diskette the current disk drive.

4. If necessary, make the diskette's root directory the current directory.

5. Type **dir** and press [Enter].

The directory list for the diskette's root directory displays. The directory list should show the two files you copied from the DOS subdirectory on the hard disk.

6. Type **move datacopy.fil \practice** and press [Enter].

DOS displays a message showing the original and target paths for the file you are moving, as shown in Figure 2-2.

7. Type **dir** and press [Enter].

A directory list for the current directory displays. Notice that there is now only one file in the current directory.

8. Type **dir \practice** and press [Enter].

Notice that the current directory now contains four files.

9. Type **move \practice*.bak ** and press [Enter].

```
A:\PRACTICE>cd..

A:\>dir

 Volume in drive A has no label
 Directory of A:\

PRACTICE     <DIR>     10-27-93   4:12p
DATACOPY FIL    61857 03-10-93   6:00a
README   TXT    61857 03-10-93   6:00a
        3 file(s)    123714 bytes
                     108544 bytes free

A:\>move datacopy.fil \practice
a:\datacopy.fil => a:\practice\datacopy.fil [ok]

A:\>
```

Figure 2-2

When you enter the MOVE command to move a file, a message appears below the command line that shows the original and target paths and whether the file was successfully transferred.

DOS displays two lines that show the original and target paths for the files you are moving from the subdirectory PRACTICE on the diskette to its root directory, as specified by the backslash character (\\) in the command.

10. Type **dir** and press Enter.

Notice that the current directory contains the two files with the BAK extension.

11. Type **dir \practice** and press Enter.

Notice that the subdirectory PRACTICE no longer contains the files with the BAK extensions.

12. Type **move *.bak \bkupdata** and press Enter.

DOS displays a prompt asking if you want the MOVE.COM program to create the subdirectory name you have specified in the command, as shown in Figure 2-3.

13. Type **y** and press Enter.

```
 Volume in drive A has no label
 Directory of A:\

PRACTICE     <DIR>     10-27-93   4:12p
DATACOPY BAK    61857 03-10-93   6:00a
README   TXT    61857 03-10-93   6:00a
README   BAK    61857 03-10-93   6:00a
        4 file(s)    185571 bytes
                     108544 bytes free

A:\>dir \practice

 Volume in drive A has no label
 Directory of A:\PRACTICE

.            <DIR>     10-27-93   4:12p
..           <DIR>     10-27-93   4:12p
DATACOPY FIL    61857 03-10-93   6:00a
PACKING  LST     2650 04-09-91   5:00a
        4 file(s)     64507 bytes
                     108544 bytes free

A:\>move *.bak \bkupdata
Make directory "a:\bkupdata"? [yn]
```

Figure 2-3

When you specify a new directory name with the MOVE command, DOS prompts you whether to create the specified directory.

DOS completes the command by creating the new directory on the diskette and moving both files with the BAK extension to the new directory.

14. Type **dir \bkupdata** and press Enter.

Notice that the new subdirectory contains the files moved from the diskette's root directory.

15. Type **cls** and press Enter to clear the screen.

Using the REN Command to Rename a File

DOS provides the internal REN command—short for "rename"—that you can use to change the name of one or more files. To use this command properly, you specify the original name and the new name when you enter the REN command, as shown in this example:

```
ren original.fil newname.doc
```

If you want to change the name of a file that is not in the current subdirectory, you must enter the path for the existing file, so that DOS knows where to find the file. An example of renaming a file in a subdirectory other than the current directory follows:

```
ren \docs\original.fil duplicat.fil
```

Changing the filenames for several files can be tricky, so use caution when attempting to rename several files. For the command to work properly, the filenames must be composed of at least one unique character and from one to seven characters that are common among the filenames. Figure 2-4 shows an example of renaming four files successfully. Notice that the original names for the four files begin with the same five characters in their filenames. The directory list that follows the command line with the REN command shows you the successful result of its operation. Because the asterisk wild card character represents the unique character in each filename, DOS replaced the characters "CHAP0" with the characters "SECTN" in each file. Incidentally, either the asterisk (*) or the question mark (?) will produce the same result in this example.

Figure 2-4

The four original files that begin with the characters "CHAP0" are renamed successfully when a wild card character is used to represent the unique character or characters in the files' names.

```
CHAP01   XYZ     82944 08-12-93  11:40a
CHAP02   XYZ     72192 08-03-93   3:39p
CHAP03   XYZ     70656 08-03-93   3:47p
CHAP04   XYZ     73216 08-03-93   4:31p
        6 file(s)     299008 bytes
                     1886208 bytes free

C:\BOOK>ren chap0*.xyz sectn*.xyz

C:\BOOK>dir

 Volume in drive C is MS-DOS_6_0
 Volume Serial Number is 1A89-8B32
 Directory of C:\BOOK

.            <DIR>      10-27-93   4:20p
..           <DIR>      10-27-93   4:20p
SECTN1   XYZ     82944 08-12-93  11:40a
SECTN2   XYZ     72192 08-03-93   3:39p
SECTN3   XYZ     70656 08-03-93   3:47p
SECTN4   XYZ     73216 08-03-93   4:31p
        6 file(s)     299008 bytes
                     1886208 bytes free

C:\BOOK>
```

The REN command will not operate successfully if you create a situation where DOS is forced to rename each file with the same file name, as would be the case if you entered the REN command shown in the following example:

```
ren chap*.xyz chapter*.xyz
```

In this case, DOS would rename the first file, CHAP01.XYZ, CHAPTER.XYZ and then display the following message:

```
Duplicate file name or file not found
```

The other original files specified in the command cannot be renamed because the new filename incorrectly replaces the unique character in each filename, forcing DOS to try to rename four files with the same file name. Be aware of this whenever you want to use the REN command to rename multiple files.

The REN command also can be used to rename several files that have the same extensions. Simply use a wild card character to represent the filenames, as shown in the following example:

```
ren *.xyz *.abc
```

Rename Files

You will use the REN command to rename files on your work diskette.

1. Make sure your computer is switched on and that the system has booted DOS properly.

2. Make sure your work diskette is in drive A (or drive B).

3. If necessary, make the drive that contains your work diskette the current disk drive.

4. If necessary, make the root directory the current directory.

5. Type **dir** and press Enter.

   In addition to the subdirectories named BKUPDATA and PRACTICE, your directory list should contain the file named README.TXT (or another file you copied from the DOS diskette that does not have the extension COM, EXE, or SYS).

6. Type **ren readme.txt sample.fil** and press Enter.

   After a few moments a new DOS prompt appears, which tells you that DOS successfully renamed the file.

(*Note*: If the file on your diskette's root directory has another name, you must enter that name for the source file in the command.)

7. Type **dir** and press Enter.

   Notice that the single file name in the current directory has been changed from README.TXT (or its original file name) to SAMPLE.FIL.

8. Type **ren \bkupdata*.bak \bkupdata*.fil** and press Enter.

DOS displays a message that tells you that the filename is invalid or cannot be found. To use the REN command properly, the file or files you want to rename must be in the current subdirectory.

9. Type **cd\bkupdata** and press Enter.

10. Type **dir** and press Enter.

11. Type **ren readme.bak sample_a.bak** and press Enter.

The file is renamed successfully, and a new DOS prompt appears.

(*Note*: If the file name README.BAK is not in the current directory on your diskette, enter the appropriate file name in the command.)

12. Type **ren datacopy.bak sample_b.bak** and press Enter.

The file is renamed successfully, and a new DOS prompt appears.

13. Type **dir** and press Enter.

Notice that both files have new names.

14. Type **cls** and press Enter to clear the screen.

15. Type **cd..** and press Enter to make the root directory current.

Removing Files from a Disk

As any PC user knows, conserving disk space, especially on hard disk drives, is very important for good work organization and efficient operation of the system. This requires that you delete files you no longer need from hard disks or diskettes periodically. DOS provides two commands that can be used to remove one or several files from any disk.

Using the DEL or ERASE Command

Both the internal DOS commands DEL, short for "delete," and ERASE work exactly the same way. You enter the command along with the file name or names—including a path, if necessary—to delete the file or files. Be very careful with either command, especially when you use a wild card character to delete more than one file. Make sure that you no longer need the files you are deleting. Although it is possible to use another DOS command, or a separate program, to retrieve data you have deleted from a disk, recovery of all of the data is never certain.

Before entering the DEL or ERASE command, use the DIR command to list the files in the disk location from which you want to delete files. This allows you to check and make sure that you do not remove a file you may still want.

When you enter either command, DOS does not give you a second chance. Once you press Enter, consider the data you have selected to be deleted permanently. However, DOS will provide you with a second chance if you enter the DEL command with wild card characters to represent all files stored in a directory, as shown in the following example:

```
del *.*
```

```
A:\BKUPDATA>cd..

A:\>c:

C:\BOOK>del *.xyz /p

C:\BOOK\SECTN1.XYZ,    Delete (Y/N)?y
C:\BOOK\SECTN2.XYZ,    Delete (Y/N)?y
C:\BOOK\SECTN3.XYZ,    Delete (Y/N)?y
C:\BOOK\SECTN4.XYZ,    Delete (Y/N)?y

C:\BOOK>
```

Figure 2-5

The /p option entered with the DEL or ERASE command forces DOS to display the name of each file specified for deletion. Then you can decide whether you want to delete each specified file.

In this case, DOS displays the following message:

```
All files in directory will be deleted!
Are you sure (Y/N)?
```

If you type **y** and press (Enter), all files in the current, or specified, directory are deleted. If you type **n** and press (Enter), the operation is canceled.

Using the Permission Option

There is a way you can verify whether to delete a file when you are in the midst of deleting multiple files. You can do this by entering the /p option (for "permission") with the DEL or ERASE command. When you enter the command, DOS displays the name of the first file that matches your specification along with a prompt asking you if you want to delete the file. Type **y** if you want to delete the displayed file or **n** if you do not. The character you type appears beside the prompt, and DOS moves on to the next file name that matches the specification in the command. Respond to each prompt for each matching file name. DOS will delete all the files for matches you respond to with a **y** and leave intact all matches you respond to with an **n**. Figure 2-5 shows an example of several files deleted with the /p option.

Delete Files

You will use the DEL command to delete multiple files from your diskette.

1. Make sure your computer is switched on and that the system has booted DOS properly.

2. Make sure your work diskette is in drive A (or drive B).

3. If necessary, make the drive that contains your work diskette the current disk drive.

4. If necessary, make the root directory the current directory.

5. Type **dir \practice** and press (Enter).

Figure 2-6

When you specify that all the files stored in a subdirectory are to be deleted, DOS displays this message. This gives you a second chance to cancel the delete operation if you change your mind.

```
A:\BKUPDATA>cd..

A:\>dir \practice

 Volume in drive A has no label
 Directory of A:\PRACTICE

.             <DIR>      10-27-93   4:12p
..            <DIR>      10-27-93   4:12p
DATACOPY FIL     61857  03-10-93   6:00a
PACKING  LST      2650  04-09-91   5:00a
         4 file(s)      64507 bytes
                       107520 bytes free

A:\>del \practice\*.*
All files in directory will be deleted!
Are you sure (Y/N)?
```

A directory list for the subdirectory PRACTICE appears. Notice that the subdirectory contains two files.

6. Type **del \practice*.*** and press [Enter].

DOS displays a message warning you that all files in the specified directory will be deleted along with a prompt asking you if you are sure you want to delete all of the files, as shown in Figure 2-6.

7. Type **y** and press [Enter].

The files are deleted from the subdirectory named PRACTICE, and a new DOS prompt appears.

8. Type **rd\practice** and press [Enter].

The subdirectory PRACTICE is removed from the diskette.

9. Type **dir \bkupdata** and press [Enter].

A directory list for the subdirectory named BKUPDATA appears. Notice that there are two files stored in this subdirectory.

10. Type **del \bkupdata*.bak /p** and press [Enter].

The path and name for the first specified file appears, and to the right of the file name is a delete prompt.

11. Type **n**

An n appears to the right of the question mark in the prompt, and the next specified file's path and name appear with another delete prompt.

12. Type **y**

A y appears to the right of the prompt, and the file is deleted from the diskette. A new DOS prompt appears.

13. Type **dir \bkupdata** and press [Enter].

Notice that the subdirectory contains only one file. The file you declined to delete remains.

14. Type **cls** and press Enter to clear the screen.

Using the TYPE Command to Display Data

Sometimes you may find yourself in situations where you need to quickly scan the contents of a file on-screen. You can do this with the internal DOS command TYPE. The TYPE command requires that you enter the name of the file you want to display on-screen, including a path, if the path is necessary, as follows:

```
type b:\textfile.doc
```

When you execute this command, the file's contents appear on-screen and scroll until all of the data stored in the file displays. If the file contains more information than can display on one screen, the information **scrolls** by, moving very quickly from the bottom of the screen to the top.

Depending on the type of data stored in the specified file, the characters that appear on screen may not make much sense to you, and you may also hear a series of "beeps" as the nonsensical characters scroll by on-screen. Do not be alarmed if this happens. All it means is that the file's data is not in text or ASCII text format.

ASCII, the acronym that stands for American Standard Code for Information Interchange, is a standard code that allows written information—letters, numbers, and symbols—to be used by computers. ASCII text format provides flexibility because this data format can be used by, or converted within, different types of applications programs.

When you enter the TYPE command with a file name for data stored in ASCII text format, the text appears on-screen, line by line, in much the way it appears in a text column on the page of a book or periodical. In other words, the characters appear on screen line by line, in one long sequence.

However, if you enter the TYPE command with a file name that stores data for a graphics file, you will see a series of characters and symbols and possibly hear numerous "beeps" when the information scrolls on screen. The information will appear meaningless to you because the data is not in ASCII text format. This can also be true for data files created in a word processor; although, you may see coherent sequences of text mixed with other nonsensical characters and symbols.

Pausing the Scrolling of Text

When you use the TYPE command to display text content in a larger file, you can use Pause to temporarily suspend scrolling. The Pause key is generally located on the right side of most keyboards. When you enter the TYPE command without any options, the information scrolls very quickly off-screen and you will not be able to read it. To use Pause, enter the TYPE command and the file name for the data you want to look at. As soon as you press Enter, press Pause immediately to stop scrolling. When you are ready to see more text, press Spacebar, or any other key, and scrolling resumes. You can continue to "pause" scrolling in this manner until all of the file's text displays.

Using the MORE Program with the TYPE Command

When you want to scan a file that contains a large amount of text data, you may find it awkward to press [Pause] and [Spacebar] (or any other key) repeatedly. Plus, this method of scrolling can make it difficult to see all of the information that scrolls. For a more convenient alternative, you can use the MORE.COM program with the TYPE command. The MORE.COM program is stored in the DOS directory, and it is often referred to as a filter.

A DOS **filter** is a special program that passes data from standard input to standard output after storing and processing the data temporarily in some way during the operation. The MORE.COM program is a filter that reads the input data, displays as many lines as will fit on the screen, and then suspends the operation until you press a key.

You use a filter program by including its name on the command line with another command, such as the TYPE command. This is called entering a **pipeline**. You do this by separating the filter's name from the rest of the command with the vertical bar character (sometimes called a pipe), including a space before and after the vertical bar character. On the screen it will look like two stacked vertical hyphens. Consider the following example:

```
type b:\textfile.doc | more
```

When you press [Enter] to execute this command, DOS displays as many of the first lines of text stored in the file TEXTFILE.DOC as will fit on one screen. You will also see the indicator "--More--"at the bottom of the screen. After you review the displayed information, press any key (usually [Spacebar]) to display the next screen of the file's content. The "--More--" indicator continues to appear at the bottom of each screen until all of the file's text has appeared. A new DOS prompt tells you that the command's operation is complete.

Display a Text File's Contents

You will use the TYPE command to display the contents of a text file on-screen.

1. Make sure your computer is switched on and that the system has booted DOS properly.

2. Make sure your work diskette is in drive A (or drive B).

3. If necessary, make the drive that contains your work diskette the current disk drive.

4. If necessary, make the root directory the current directory.

5. Type **type sample.fil** and press [Enter].

    The text stored in the specified file begins to scroll from the bottom of the screen to the top.

6. Press [Pause].

    The scrolling stops.

7. Press [Spacebar] or any other key.

    The scrolling resumes.

8. Press [Ctrl]-**c**.

```
README.TXT

NOTES ON MS-DOS 6
=================

This file provides important information not included in the
MICROSOFT MS-DOS 6 USER'S GUIDE or in MS-DOS Help.

This file is divided into the following major sections:

1. Setup
2. MemMaker and Memory Management
3. Windows
4. Hardware Compatibility with MS-DOS 6
5. Microsoft Programs
6. Third-Party Programs
7. DoubleSpace

If the subject you need information about doesn't appear in
this file, you might find it in one of the following text
files included with MS-DOS:

× OS2.TXT, which describes how to remove and save data on your
-- More --
```

Figure 2-7

When you pipeline the MORE.COM program with the TYPE command, DOS displays an indicator that tells you more text information will appear when you press any key.

The command is aborted, and a new DOS prompt appears.

9. Type **type sample.fil | more** and press ⟨Enter⟩.

   The first 23 lines of text appear, scrolling pauses, and the "More" indicator appears, as shown in Figure 2-7.

10. Press ⟨Spacebar⟩ or any other key.

    The next screen of text scrolls into view and pauses.

11. Press ⟨Spacebar⟩ or any other key.

12. Press ⟨Ctrl⟩-**c**.

    The command is aborted, and a new DOS prompt appears.

13. Type **cls** and press ⟨Enter⟩ to clear the screen.

Using the PRINT Command to Print a Text File

In much the same way the TYPE command displays text characters on-screen, the external DOS command PRINT sends a file's contents to a printer connected to the computer. If the printed information is to be intelligible, the file you specify with the PRINT command should be in ASCII text format. Many applications programs allow you to "print" data to a print file, which stores the information in ASCII text format.

The PRINT command executes a memory-resident program. A **memory-resident program** is loaded into the computer's memory where it remains until power to the computer is switched off. Memory-resident programs occupy as little memory as possible so they can remain active while the computer is doing other work. Then when you need to use the memory-resident program, it is ready to go to work.

You load the PRINT program into memory by entering the PRINT command the first time at the DOS prompt, along with the printer's name. For most personal computers this is LPT1. LPT1 is a device name for the connection between the printer and the personal computer. If you have more than one printer connected to the system, you can use the device names LPT2 or LPT3. The format for the command is as follows:

```
print /d:lpt1
```

When you enter this command, DOS loads the PRINT.EXE program into memory. The "/d:" part of the command is an option that tells DOS that the following characters represent a device name. Once the command is entered, it is ready for you to use when you need it. To use the program, type the PRINT command again, followed by the name of the file containing the data you want to send to the printer.

The advantage of using the PRINT program is that it gives you what is called background printing. **Background printing** allows your printer to print data while using only the amount of the personal computer's resources necessary to print. This frees most of the computer's power to work on other things while data is printing. Otherwise, the printing process can slow your computer's processing speed significantly. Many applications programs are equipped with a background printing feature, so depending on the programs you work with it may not be necessary to use the DOS PRINT program.

Print a Text File

You will load the PRINT program into memory, and then you will print a text file.

1. Make sure your computer is switched on and that the system has booted DOS properly.

2. Make sure your work diskette is in drive A (or drive B).

3. If necessary, make the drive that contains your work diskette the current disk drive.

4. If necessary, make the root directory the current directory.

5. Make sure there is a printer connected properly to your system.

6. Check that the printer has paper, that the paper is aligned properly, and that the printer is on and ready to print.

7. Type **print /d:lpt1** and press Enter.

   DOS displays a message telling you that the resident part of the program is installed (loaded into memory) and that the print queue is empty.

8. Type **copy c:\dos60\packing.lst** and press Enter.

   The text file PACKING.LST, stored in the DOS program subdirectory, copies to the current root directory on the diskette in drive A (or drive B).

(*Note*: If you are using an earlier version of DOS and/or your working copy of DOS is stored on a diskette in drive A (diskette drive systems), you may have to specify another path and/or text file that is appropriate for your system.)

9. Type **print packing.lst** and press Enter.

   The text content stored in the file named PACKING.LST is sent to the print queue and should begin printing. DOS displays a message telling you that the specified file is printing.

(*Note*: If the text does not print, check that your printer is properly connected to the system and that the file name you specified exists in the specified directory. If you cannot print a text file successfully, check with your instructor or a technical support person.)

10. Type **cls** and press ⎡Enter⎤ to clear the screen.

Checking a Disk

There will likely be times when you want to view status information for your hard disk or a diskette containing data. You can do this with the external DOS command CHKDSK. You can specify the disk for which you want a status report by including its drive specification with the command or you can obtain a status report on the current disk by entering the command alone. An example of the status report that the CHKDSK command gives you is shown in Figure 2-8.

Notice that the same first two lines that appear on-screen when you enter the DIR command also appear when you enter the CHKDSK command. These lines provide the volume label, the date and time the disk was formatted, and the volume serial number assigned by the FORMAT.COM program (DOS 4.0 and later).

Following the first two lines, the status report shows the total disk space and the quantities of disk space used by directories, hidden files, and user files. User files store programs you write or work you save when you use applications software. Hidden files are special DOS program files. The amount of space available for more data is also shown on the status report.

The next three lines display similar information on the disk's allocation units. **Allocation units** refer to the number of storage areas or blocks that DOS reserves for storing specific amounts of information. Finally, the last two lines give you a separate status report on the total amount of memory available in your system and the amount that is free or available currently. Even though this additional memory information has nothing to do with the disk you are checking, it can be helpful to know how much memory is occupied currently and how much is available for your work.

```
Volume MS-DOS_6_0  created 04-09-1993 10:33p
Volume Serial Number is 1A89-8B3Z
Errors found, F parameter not specified
Corrections will not be written to disk

    25 lost allocation units found in 2 chains.
    51200 bytes disk space would be freed

71067648 bytes total disk space
 4270080 bytes in 4 hidden files
  186368 bytes in 63 directories
64235520 bytes in 2173 user files
  174080 bytes in bad sectors
 2150400 bytes available on disk

    2048 bytes in each allocation unit
   34701 total allocation units on disk
    1050 available allocation units on disk

  655360 total bytes memory
  562352 bytes free

C:\>
```

Figure 2-8

This is an example of the status report that appears when you use the CHKDSK command to check the status of a disk.

Figure 2-9

The message shown here at the top of the screen is an example of a disk space allocation error that can be detected when you check a hard disk with the CHKDSK command. When you use the /f option with the CHKDSK command, DOS displays the message shown at the bottom of the screen. If you type **y** and press Enter, the CHKDSK program creates a file for each "lost chain" of unaccounted for allocation units.

```
     25 lost allocation units found in 2 chains.
     51200 bytes disk space would be freed

71067648 bytes total disk space
 4270080 bytes in 4 hidden files
  186368 bytes in 63 directories
64235520 bytes in 2173 user files
  174080 bytes in bad sectors
 2150400 bytes available on disk

    2048 bytes in each allocation unit
   34701 total allocation units on disk
    1050 available allocation units on disk

  655360 total bytes memory
  562352 bytes free

C:\>chkdsk /f

Volume MS-DOS_6_0  created 04-09-1993 10:33p
Volume Serial Number is 1A89-8B32

     25 lost allocation units found in 2 chains.
Convert lost chains to files (Y/N)?
```

Using the /f Option

Although it is a rare occurrence, sometimes you might see an additional message in the CHKDSK status report that indicates a disk space allocation error. This message appears after the first two lines of the report and before the lines containing the disk space quantities, as shown in Figure 2-9.

In a nutshell, this message means that the CHKDSK program has encountered disk space allocation units that appear to be used but do not appear to be associated with a file. Sometimes this occurs when power to the computer is switched off while one or more applications programs are running with opened temporary files. Most of the time this has no impact on your data; however, sometimes, you can lose some valuable data in this situation.

If you see such a message, it is very likely that the CHKDSK program can fix this problem, which will free disk space occupied by the unaccounted for allocation units. However, you must include the /f option (for "fix") to give the CHKDSK program the OK to do so. For example, you would enter the command as follows:

```
chkdsk c: /f
```

If there are unaccounted for allocation units, the CHKDSK program displays the message shown at the bottom of Figure 2-9. This prompt gives you the option of having the CHKDSK program create files that you can check (with the TYPE command) to see if they contain data you have lost. Often the data in these files (lost chains) appears as random characters that are not useful to you. If you think the data is of no use, you can type **n** and press Enter. The data is not saved, and the disk space occupied by the allocation units is freed. Otherwise you can type **y** and press Enter to tell CHKDSK to create the files.

The program creates a file for each lost unit. The filenames for these files include a number to distinguish them. For example, in the situation shown in Figures 2-8 and 2-9, the CHKDSK program would create the following two files in the root directory for drive C:

```
FILE000.CHK
FILE001.CHK
```

```
PRINT queue is empty

A:\>copy c:\dos60\packing.lst
        1 file(s) copied

A:\>print packing.lst


  A:\PACKING.LST is currently being printed

A:\>chkdsk

    362496 bytes total disk space
      1024 bytes in 1 directories
    128000 bytes in 3 user files
    233472 bytes available on disk

      1024 bytes in each allocation unit
       354 total allocation units on disk
       228 available allocation units on disk

    655360 total bytes memory
    562352 bytes free

A:\>
```

Figure 2-10

You should see a status report similar to this when you enter the CHKDSK command to check your work diskette.

You can look at the data stored in these files either by using the TYPE command or by opening the file in a word processing program. If the files contain data you do not want, simply delete them with the DEL or ERASE command. Because these files occupy disk space just like any other file, deleting them will free more disk space for your work.

Check a Disk's Status

You will use the CHKDSK command to check the status of disks.

1. Make sure your computer is switched on and that the system has booted DOS properly.

2. Make sure your work diskette is in drive A (or drive B).

3. If necessary, make the drive that contains your work diskette the current disk drive.

4. Type **chkdsk** and press Enter.

   A status report for the diskette in the current drive appears, as shown in Figure 2-10.

5. If your system has a hard disk drive, type **chkdsk c:** and press Enter.

   A status report for the hard disk drive displays.

6. If the status report that appeared after you did step 5 indicated the presence of errors, enter the command again using the /f option. Then use the TYPE command to display the contents of one of the files that the CHKDSK program created to fix the errors (for example, FILE0000.CHK).

7. Type **cls** and press Enter to clear the screen.

Using the MS-DOS Shell

The MS-DOS Shell program is available with versions 4.0, 5.0, and 6.0 of the DOS software. A **shell program** operates as an additional layer that surrounds, or works in conjunction with, the other programs you use on a personal computer. The DOS Shell program provides a graphic interface that is an alternative to the text mode command line that you have been working with up to this point.

Figure 2-11

When you enter the DOSSHELL command to start the DOS Shell program, a screen similar to this appears. The DOS Shell screen displays icons, list areas, and the program's menu bar.

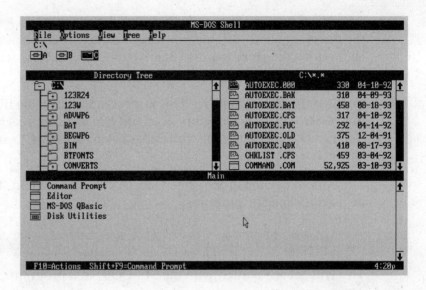

A **graphic interface** is an environment that allows you to use a mouse (or the keyboard) to select options from menus on-screen without having to use the keyboard to type commands. Graphic interfaces also often include **icons**, which are small graphic pictures or symbols that you can point to with the mouse pointer and select by clicking a mouse button. This action carries out an operation or a command represented by the icon.

Loading the MS-DOS Shell

To start the MS-DOS Shell program, type the command DOSSHELL at the DOS prompt and press [Enter]. After the program is loaded into the computer's memory, a screen like the one shown in Figure 2-11 appears. The screen may appear different on different personal computers. Like the DOS command line, you can use the Shell program to access other applications or to perform DOS operations. The Shell program remains resident in memory so that its options are available to you while you work.

Using Command Menus

Notice in Figure 2-11 that the Shell screen is divided into several areas. At the very top of the screen is a **menu bar**. You can use the mouse to click on a menu name, which causes the menu to display by appearing to "drop down" from the menu bar. On these drop-down menus are command options that you can select to perform a particular operation. For example, the File menu contains many of the commands you have learned to use in this tutorial, including Copy, Move, Rename, Delete, and so forth.

If you want to select menus and menu options with the keyboard, you can do so by pressing [Alt] and then pressing the first letter in the menu's name. When the menu appears, you can type the highlighted or underlined letter—called a **mnemonic letter**—in a command's name to select it. For example, you can exit the Shell program by pressing [Alt] and then typing **fx**. The "**f**" and the "**x**" are the mnemonic letters in the File menu name and the Exit command, respectively.

Below the menu bar is a selection of the available disk drives on the computer system. The highlighted drive specification icon indicates the current disk drive. Similarly, the Directory Tree portion of the screen lists the subdirectory names available on the current disk. If a plus sign (+) appears in a file folder icon or enclosed in square brackets beside the directory name, this means that the directory contains other subdirectories. You can click on the directory name to display the subdirectory names stored in the selected, or current, subdirectory.

To the right of the Directory Tree is an area that lists the file names in the current directory. Notice that the Directory Tree and File List areas each have a **vertical scroll bar**. You can use the mouse to scroll either list and display the rest of the directory or file names not shown.

The bottom portion of the screen labeled "Main" contains DOS program names that can be used for specific purposes.

Start and Exit the MS-DOS Shell

You will get acquainted with the MS-DOS Shell program.

(*Note*: If you are using a version of DOS earlier than version 4.0, you will not be able to complete this exercise.)

1. Make sure your computer is switched on and that the system has booted DOS properly.

2. Make sure your work diskette is in drive A (or drive B).

3. If necessary, make the hard disk drive the current disk drive.

4. Type **cd\dos60** and press Enter.

(*Note*: If your DOS program files are stored in a directory with another name, enter that name instead for step 4.)

5. Type **dosshell** and press Enter.

    The DOS Shell program loads and the DOS Shell screen appears.

6. Press Alt.

    The menu bar is active.

7. Press Tab.

    The disk drive area is now active.

8. Press ← or →, as necessary, to highlight the icon for disk drive A.

9. Press Enter.

    Disk drive A is now the current disk drive. Notice that the directory name BKUPDATA appears in the Directory Tree area.

10. Press Tab and then press ↓.

    The directory name BKUPDATA highlights in the Directory Tree area.

11. Press Enter.

    Notice that the single file name stored in this subdirectory appears in the File List area.

Figure 2-12

The File drop-down menu
appears when you select the File
command on the menu bar.
Drop-down menus on the DOS
Shell screen contain selections of
DOS command options.

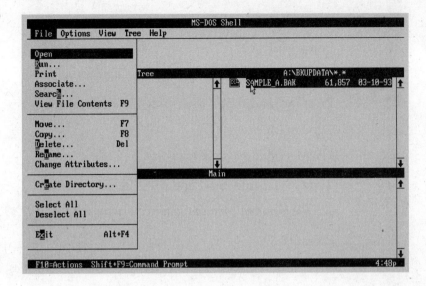

12. Press [Alt] and then type **f**.

The File drop-down menu appears, as shown in Figure 2-12. Notice that the Copy command does not have an underlined mnemonic letter. This means that the command is not available because the File List area was not active when you selected the File menu.

13. Press [Esc].

The File menu disappears.

14. Press [Tab].

The File List area is now active.

15. Press [Alt] and then type **f** to display the File menu.

Notice that the Copy command is now available.

16. Type **c** (or press [F8]) to select the Copy command.

The Copy File dialog box appears, as shown in Figure 2-13.

Figure 2-13

When you select the Copy
command on the File menu with
the File List area active, a Copy
File dialog box appears with the
selected file names listed. You
can specify another disk location
and/or file name for the target
file.

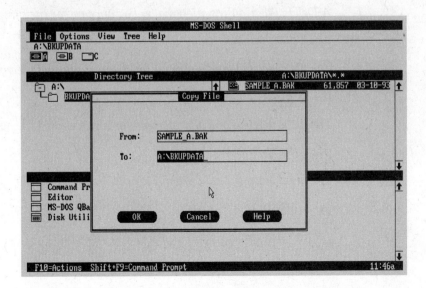

17. Press ⟶ and then press Bksp 8 times.

18. Press Enter.

    The file is copied to the diskette's root directory.

19. Press Alt and type **f** to display the File menu.

20. Type **m** (or press F7).

    The Move File dialog box appears.

21. Type **a:\sample_b.txt** and press Enter.

    The file is moved from the subdirectory named BKUPDATA to the diskette's root directory.

22. Press ↑.

    Notice that the diskette's root directory contains four files.

23. Press ↓ and then press Del.

    The Delete Directory Confirmation dialog box appears with the Yes command button ready for selection.

24. Press Enter.

    The subdirectory named BKUPDATA is deleted (removed) from the diskette.

25. Press Tab to activate the File List area.

26. Press Alt and then type **f** to display the File menu.

27. Type **s** to choose the Select All command.

    The three file names in the current directory are highlighted.

28. Press Del.

    The Delete File dialog box appears.

29. Press Enter to select the OK command button.

    A Delete File Confirmation dialog box appears for the first file.

30. Press Enter.

    The file is deleted, and a prompt for the next selected file appears.

31. Press Enter.

    The file is deleted, and a prompt for the next selected file appears.

32. Press Enter.

    The file is deleted, and a prompt for the next selected file appears.

33. Press Enter.

    All four files are deleted. The diskette is now empty.

34. Press [Alt] and type **f** to display the File menu.

35. Type **x** to select the Exit command.

A DOS prompt appears after you exit the DOS Shell program. Notice that the current disk drive is the same drive that was current when the DOS Shell program was active.

Command Summary

Internal Commands

COPY	Copies data from one or more files to files with the same file names in other directories or on other disks; or copies data from one or more files to files with different file names to any disk location, including the current directory.
DEL *or* ERASE	Deletes (removes) one or more files from a specified disk location.
REN	Changes the name or names for one or more files in the current directory.
TYPE	Displays text data on-screen for a specified file.

External Commands

CHKDSK	Provides a status report for a specified disk that includes total available disk space, disk space occupied by various types of files, and free disk space available for additional data. Can also detect unaccounted for allocation units and create files for the extraneous data when the /f option is provided with the command.
MORE	Filters standard input from another DOS command and provides standard output so that information fills a single screen and waits for user input before scrolling additional information.
MOVE	Moves data in one or more files from one directory or disk to another, changes the name or names of the moved files, and/or creates a new subdirectory while moving files.
PRINT	Sends text data directly to a printer connected to the system after the PRINT program is resident in memory.
DOSSHELL	Loads the DOS Shell program, which provides a graphic interface for selecting DOS commands.

Review Questions

1. Is a target path necessary if you want to copy files from another disk to the current subdirectory? Explain your answer.

2. What is the primary difference between the result of an operation carried out by the COPY command and the result obtained with the MOVE command (DOS 6.0 only)? Which command is better for backing up data? Why?

3. What situation should you avoid when you want to change the names of several files with the REN command?

4. Which option can you use with the DEL or ERASE command to verify each and every file you want to delete when you are deleting several files?

5. What additional information does the CHKDSK command provide that is not provided by the DIR command?

6. Can you think of two benefits the DOS Shell program provides over the DOS command line interface?

Application Projects

1. Copy the files named PACKING.LST and README.TXT from the DOS program subdirectory to a properly formatted and empty diskette. If these files are unavailable to you, see your instructor for some files you can use for DOS operations. Copy these files so they are stored with new extensions in the same directory. If you are using DOS version 6.0, move the two original files on the diskette to a new directory on the diskette named ORIGINAL.

2. Make sure you do Application 1 before you do this application. Copy the two files in the diskette's root directory to the same directory, and then copy the two files in the subdirectory ORIGINAL to that directory. Both the root directory and the subdirectory ORIGINAL will contain four files. Use the CHKDSK command to note the diskette's current disk space allocation. Next, load the DOS Shell program, and use the appropriate File menu options to delete the files in the subdirectory ORIGINAL and then remove the subdirectory from the diskette. Exit the DOS Shell program, and then use the CHKDSK command to check the status of the diskette.

3. Figure 2-14 shows five commands that were not entered correctly. Describe the problem with each command that caused DOS to return the error messages shown. How can each be corrected to work properly?

```
C:\BOOK>ren chaptr*.upf 1chapter.upf
Duplicate file name or file not found

C:\>del chaptr01.upf
File not found

C:\BOOK>copy *.* *.upf
CHAPTR01.UPF
File cannot be copied onto itself
        0 file(s) copied

C:\BOOK>move *.upf
Required parameter missing

C:\BOOK>chkdsk d: /f
Invalid drive specification
Invalid media type

C:\BOOK>
```

Figure 2-14

For Application Project 3, describe the reasons why the five commands shown here did not work; also describe how they can be corrected so they do work.

4. Describe exactly what will occur when the following commands are entered.

    a. C:\>copy *.bat \bat*.old

    b. A:\>copy c:\dos60*.com

    c. C:\DOCS>del *.bak

    d. B:\>ren ???BUDGT.* ???EXPNS.*

    e. C:\CLIENTS>move *.95 \oldclnts*.96

    f. A:>chkdsk c: /f

    g. C:\MEMOS>type libbymem.txt | more

APPENDIX: DOS 6 COMMAND SUMMARY

Internal Commands

CLS	Clears the screen of information and displays a single DOS prompt in the upper-left corner
DIR	Displays a listing of files, subdirectories, and other disk information for the current or specified disk and/or directory
MKDIR (MD)	Creates a subdirectory
CHDIR (CD)	Changes the current, or default, subdirectory
RMDIR (RD)	Removes, or deletes, a subdirectory
COPY	Copies data from one or more files to files with the same file names in other directories or on other disks; or copies data from one or more files to files with different file names to any disk location, including the current directory.
DEL *or* ERASE	Deletes (removes) one or more files from a specified disk location.
REN	Changes the name or names for one or more files in the current directory.
TYPE	Displays text data on-screen for a specified file.

External Commands

FORMAT.COM	Formats a diskette so it can be used to store data
CHKDSK	Provides a status report for a specified disk that includes total available disk space, disk space occupied by various types of files, and free disk space available for additional data. Can also detect unaccounted for allocation units and create files for the extraneous data when the /f option is provided with the command.
MORE	Filters standard input from another DOS command and provides standard output so that information fills a single screen and waits for user input before scrolling additional information.
MOVE	Moves data in one or more files from one directory or disk to another, changes the name or names of the moved files, and/or creates a new subdirectory while moving files.
PRINT	Sends text data directly to a printer connected to the system after the PRINT program is resident in memory.
DOSSHELL	Loads the DOS Shell program, which provides a graphic interface for selecting DOS commands.

GLOSSARY

allocation units designated storage areas, or blocks, that DOS reserves for storing specific amounts of information

applications software a program designed to perform a specific task, such as word processing

ASCII (American Standard Code for Information Interchange) a standard code that allows computers to use written information (letters, numbers, and symbols), and that provides for convenient data transfer between different types of applications programs

asterisk a wild card character (*) used to represent any string of consecutive characters in a file name's filename or extension

background printing the printing of data using only the necessary amount of a personal computer's resources, leaving most of the computer's power free to work on other things at the same time

boot a process in which operating system software is loaded into random access memory

bootstrap loader a built-in start-up program that, during the booting process, reads the part of a disk containing special DOS instructions for setting up the operating system and loading it into the computer's RAM

branch the hierarchical structure (tree structure) characteristic of the directory system on a disk

command a filename for a program file, such as PRINT or COPY; *see also* external command, internal command

command interpreter the COMMAND.COM file, which stores internal commands, displays the DOS prompt, waits for the user to enter a command, reads the command into memory, and carries out assigned instructions

data file a file that stores information electronically and that is created by a user using an applications program

directory a special file used to group a set of files related in some way meaningful to a user; often used interchangeably with *subdirectory*

disk a common storage medium; a flat, round object with a magnetic coating. It stores the electronic impulses that represent data

disk drive configuration the type of disk drive devices with which a system is equipped, including hard disk drives and diskette drives

disk operating system (DOS) operating system software, developed by Microsoft Corporation for the IBM PC and IBM-compatible personal computers, that controls a computer's operating environment, including the transfer of data between the computer and disk drives; *see also* MS-DOS, PC-DOS

diskette a storage device made up of a thin platter encased in a flexible or a hard plastic jacket. It allows data to be moved from one computer to another and to be backed up from storage on a hard disk drive

diskette drive an input-output device that facilitates the use of diskettes for reading and writing information; also called a floppy disk drive

DOS *see* disk operating system

DOS prompt an on-screen symbol or marker that identifies the command line where a user types a command for a DOS operation or to start an application program

drive name a single letter that identifies a disk drive and distinguishes it from other disk drives in a system

drive specification a drive letter and a colon (:) that identifies a disk drive and that can be entered as a command to change the current drive

executable said of a file or command that is written in a specific programming language to allow the computer to perform one or more specific tasks—such as loading and running applications software—when the filename portion is entered at the DOS prompt

extension the part of a file name that is made up of one to three characters and separated from the filename by a period

external command a DOS program file, stored on a hard disk or on a diskette, that has the COM or EXE extension in its file name

file name a name that is used to identify a data file or a program file, and that is made up of a filename and an extension

file server the computer in a Local Area Network, which contains a high-capacity hard disk drive and stores applications programs and data files that can be accessed by any number of user terminals connected to the network

file specification an expression or syntax that identifies the exact location for a set of data, including the disk drive, directories, and the file's filename and extension; *see also* path

filename the first part of a file name, made up of one to eight characters and separated from the extension by a period

filter a special program that passes data from standard input to standard output after storing and processing the data temporarily in some way

formatting a disk-preparation process that divides the disk's surface into sectors and structures usable portions of the disk around any defective areas detected

graphic interface an environment in which a mouse (or keyboard) or other pointing device can be used to select options directly on the screen

hard disk a storage device made up of metallic platters in a sealed housing. It may be mounted inside the computer, or it may be removable. It contains higher storage capacity than a diskette

IBM DOS *see* PC-DOS

icon a small graphic picture or symbol that a user can point to with a mouse pointer, and select by clicking a mouse button, to carry out an operation or command

input/output (I/O) device a peripheral device that sends and/or receives data that the computer works with by either reading the data from or writing the data to a diskette or other medium

internal command a command that executes instructions stored in the COMMAND.COM program file, which DOS keeps resident in memory at all times after the operating system software is successfully booted on a personal computer

Local Area Network (LAN) a group of personal computers that function as terminals connected to a central file server, and that allow users to share data and peripheral devices

memory-resident program a program that is loaded into a computer's memory and remains there until power to the computer is switched off, and that occupies as little memory as possible but is ready for use when needed

menu bar a bar across the top of the screen of a drop-down menu system, such as DOS Shell, that displays the types of commands available to a user

mnemonic letter a highlighted or underlined letter in a menu name or command, which represents the letter key that a user can press to display the menu or select (execute) the command

motherboard the computer's main system board, where the central processing unit and the memory are located; also called a *system board*

MS-DOS DOS versions distributed by Microsoft Corporation for IBM-compatible personal computers manufactured by companies other than IBM

operating environment the user, applications software, and hardware that make up a computer system

operating system a set of computer programs that control the computer's operation and manage the operating environment

parameter additional information necessary for DOS to carry out a procedure specified in a particular program file

parent directory the directory (root directory or other subdirectory) in which a subdirectory exists

partitioned a condition in which a hard disk drive is set up to function as two or more separate drives

path the course from the root directory of a specified drive through any subdirectories to a file specification that identifies the exact location of a set of data (data file)

path name a description that DOS can interpret to locate a file

PC-DOS DOS distributed by IBM for its personal computer and Personal System/2 product lines; also called *IBM DOS*

peripheral device any machine, such as a printer or a monitor, that is not physically part of a computer but that is connected and operates in combination with the computer

pipeline a form of command entry in which a filter program is included on the command line with a DOS command and is separated from the DOS command by a split vertical bar symbol (|) between two spaces

program file a file that contains programming instructions that command the computer to perform one or more specific tasks

question mark a wild card character (?) that represents any single character in a filename or extension

root directory the first or main directory on a disk, which also establishes the total amount of disk space available for storing data

scroll the movement of information on screen in which each line moves quickly from the bottom of the screen to the top as all specified information appears

sector an area of a disk in which DOS stores data

shell program a graphic interface, provided with DOS 4.0, 5.0, and 6.0, that is an alternative to the text mode command line and that works in conjunction with other programs used on a personal computer

storage device a physical component that receives data electronically, holds the data for an indefinite period, and then supplies the data upon command when the user and the computer need the data

subdirectory a directory within a root directory or any other directory, that is created by a user to group files that are related in some meaningful way to the user; often used interchangeably with *directory*

system board *see* motherboard

system disk a diskette containing the essential program files used to boot DOS; can be used for booting DOS on a system without a hard disk drive

vertical scroll bar a graphic interface device that allows a user to use a mouse to scroll information appearing in a boxed list or window

volume label a name assigned to a diskette that is made up of one to eleven characters

warm boot the process of booting operating system software on a computer that has the power switched on. Carried out by pressing the Control key, the Alternate key, and the Delete key simultaneously.

wild card a character included in a file specification on the command line; used to indicate several files in a specific disk location for an operation. *See also* asterisk, question mark

INDEX

A

allocation units, 50, 51
    unaccounted for, 51
Application Projects, 32–33, 58–59
applications software, 2
ASCII text format, 46, 48
asterisk (*) wild card character, 29, 37, 41
    See also wild card characters

B

background printing, 49
    See also printing files
booting DOS, 6–9
    with cold boot, 6
    defined, 6
    with diskette drive, 7, 9–10
    with hard disk configuration, 7, 9
    on LANs, 8
    procedure for, 9–10
    with warm boot, 8

C

CD (CHDIR) command, 21–24, 32
    backslash and, 22
    function of, 21, 22
CHKDSK command, 50–52, 57
    disk space allocation error, 51
    /f (fix) option, 51–52
    function of, 50
    status report, 50
    using, 52
CHKDSK program, 51–52
    creating files option, 51
CLS command, 15, 18, 19, 32
COMMAND.COM file, 14, 15
command interpreter, 14
commands
    case of, 11
    classifications for, 14
    entering, 11
    external, 15
    incorrect, 11
    internal, 14
    typing mistakes and, 11
    understanding, 14–15
    wild card characters and, 29–30
commands, list of
    CD (CHDIR), 21–24, 32
    CHKDSK, 50–52, 57
    CLS, 15, 18, 19, 32
    COPY, 14, 34–38, 57
    DEL (ERASE), 38, 57
    DIR, 24–28, 32
    DOSSHELL, 53, 57
    FORMAT, 15–19, 32
    MD (MKDIR), 20–22, 32
    MORE, 57
    MOVE, 38–41
    PRINT, 48–50, 57

RD (RMDIR), 30–31, 32
REN, 38, 41–43, 47
TYPE, 46–48, 57
COPY command, 14, 34–38, 57
    using, 34–38
Copy File dialog box, 55–56
copying files, 34–38, 57
    to another disk, 35
    DIR command and, 36
    from DOS Shell, 55–56
    multiple files, 36
    on diskette drive systems, 37–38
    on hard drive systems, 36–37
    procedure for, 36–38
    to same disk, 35
`Ctrl`-`Alt`-`Del`, 8, 9, 10
`Ctrl`-c, 47, 48

D

data files, 11
    program files and, 13–14
date, entering, 7–8, 9
DEL (ERASE) command, 38, 57
    DIR command before, 43
    entering, 43–44
    /p (permission) option, 44
    using, 43–44
    wild card characters and, 43–44
Delete Directory Confirmation dialog box, 56
Delete File dialog box, 56
deleting files, 43–46, 56, 57
    procedure for, 44–46
    using DEL (ERASE) command, 43–44
    using /p (permission) option, 44
DIR command, 24–28, 32
    /p (pause) option, 26
    /w (wide) option, 27
    backslash and, 24
    before DEL (ERASE) command, 43
    function of, 24
    illustrated example, 25
    listing files with, 24–26
    on diskette drive systems, 25–26
        parameters and, 28–29
    on hard disk drive systems, 25
        parameters and, 27–28
    parameters, 26–29
        combining, 27, 28
directories, 19–24
    creating, 39, 40–41
    displaying list of, 25–26, 32
    example of, 20
    parent, 20
    root, 19, 20, 22–23, 24
    types of, 19
    See also files; paths; subdirectories
disk drives, 3
    changing, 10–12
    checking, 50–52
    configurations of, 5

floppy. *See* diskette drives
hard. *See* hard disks
managing space on, 19
names of, 11
specification, 10
using, 10–11
diskette drives, 5–6
    booting DOS with, 7, 9–10
    I/O device, 5
    name of, 5–6
    types of, 5
    See also diskette drive systems
diskette drive systems
    copying on, 37–38
    directory lists on, 25–26, 28–29
    formatting disks on, 19
diskettes, 3–4
    capacity of, 4
    formatting, 15–19, 32
    sectors of, 15
    types of, 4
    volume label, 17
    write-protecting, 4–5
    See also diskette drives
disk operating system. *See* DOS
DOS
    booting, 6–10
    commands, 11, 14–15
    compatibility, 3
    defined, 3
    device names, 13
    filter, 47
    function of, 1
    role of, v
    types of, 3
    version of, 3
DOS prompt, 9
    understanding, 10
DOSSHELL command, 53, 57

E

ERASE command. *See* DEL (ERASE) command
extensions, file name, 12
    BAT, 14
    COM, 13, 15
    commands and, 14
    examples of, 13–14
    EXE, 13, 15
    SYS, 13, 14

F

file names, 11–13
    defined, 12
    device names and, 13
    duplicate data and, 35
    extensions for, 12, 13, 14
    filename for, 12
    parts of, 12
    renaming multiple, 41
    rules for, 12–13